FILM
SCRIPTS

PIERROT LE FOU

a film by

Jean-Luc Godard

English translation and description of action
by Peter Whitehead

Simon and Schuster, New York

Published by Simon and Schuster
Rockefeller Center, 630 Fifth Avenue
New York, New York 10020
First printing

SBN 671-20448-3
Library of Congress Catalog Card Number: 75-92178

General Editor: Sandra Wake

Manufactured in Great Britain by Villiers Publications Ltd,
London NW 5

CONTENTS

ACKNOWLEDGMENTS

We wish to thank Gala Films in London and *L'Avant-Scène du Cinéma* in Paris for loaning us prints of the film.

The *Cahiers du Cinema* interview *Let's Talk About Pierrot* was published in the book *Jean-Luc Godard par Jean-Luc Godard*, Editions Pierre Belfond, Paris, 1968. The text which appears here is taken from the English translation of the book by Tom Milne, which will be published under the title *Godard on Godard* by Thames & Hudson and Viking Press in 1970.

LET'S TALK ABOUT *PIERROT*

Interview with Jean-Luc Godard

CAHIERS — *What exactly was the starting-point for* Pierrot le Fou?

GODARD — A *Lolita*-style novel whose rights I had bought two years earlier. The film was to have been made with Sylvie Vartan. She refused. Instead I made *Bande à part*. Then I tried to set the film up again with Anna Karina and Richard Burton. Burton, alas, had become too Hollywood. In the end the whole thing was changed by the casting of Anna and Belmondo. I thought about *You Only Live Once;* and instead of the *Lolita* or *La Chienne* kind of couple, I wanted to tell the story of the last romantic couple, the last descendants of *La Nouvelle Héloïse, Werther* and *Hermann and Dorothea*.

CAHIERS — *This sort of romanticism is disconcerting today, just as the romanticism of* La Règle du Jeu *was at the time.*

GODARD — One is always disconcerted by something or other. One Sunday afternoon a couple of weeks ago I saw *October* again at the Cinémathèque. The audience was composed entirely of children, going to the cinema for the first time, so they reacted as if it was the first film they had seen. They may have been disconcerted by the cinema, but not by the film. For instance, they were not at all put out by the rapid, synthetic montage. When they now see a Verneuil film they will be disconcerted because they will think, ' But there are fewer shots than in *October* '. Let's take another example from America, where television is much more cut up and fragmented than it is in France. There, one doesn't just watch a film from beginning to end; one sees fifteen shows at the same time while doing something else, not to mention the commercials (if *they* were missing, that *would* disconcert). *Hiroshima* and *Lola Montès* went down much better on TV in America than in the cinemas.

CAHIERS — Pierrot, *in any case, will please children. They can dream while watching it.*

5

GODARD — The film, alas, is banned to children under eighteen. Reason? Intellectual and moral anarchy [*sic*].

CAHIERS — *There is a good deal of blood in* Pierrot.

GODARD — Not blood, red. At any rate, I find it difficult to talk about the film. I can't say I didn't work it out, but I didn't pre-think it. Everything happened at once : it is a film in which there was no writing, editing or mixing — well, one day! Bonfanti knew nothing of the film and he mixed the soundtrack without preparation. He reacted with his knobs like a pilot faced by air-pockets. This was very much in key with the spirit of the film. So the construction came at the same time as the detail. It was a series of structures which immediately dovetailed one with another.

CAHIERS — *Did* Bande à part *and* Alphaville *happen in the same way?*

GODARD — Ever since my first film, I have always said I am going to prepare the script more carefully, and each time I see yet another chance to improvise, to do it all in the shooting, without applying the cinema to something. My impression is that when someone like Demy or Bresson shoots a film, he has an idea of the world he is trying to apply to the cinema, or else — which comes to the same thing — an idea of cinema which he applies to the world. The cinema and the world are moulds for matter, but in *Pierrot* there is neither mould nor matter.

CAHIERS — *There seems at times to be an interaction between certain situations which existed at the moment of shooting and the film itself. For instance, when Anna Karina walks along the beach saying ' What am I to do? I don't know what to do . . .' as if, at this moment, she hadn't known what to do, had said so, and you had filmed her.*

GODARD — It didn't happen that way, but maybe it comes to the same thing. If I had seen a girl walking along the shore saying ' I don't know what to do ', I might well have thought this was a good scene; and, starting from there, imagined what came before and after. Instead of speaking of the sky, speaking of the sea, which isn't the same thing; instead of being sad, being gay, instead of dancing, having a scene with people eating, which again isn't the same thing; but the final effect would have been the same. In fact it happened like that not for this scene, but another in which Anna says to Belmondo ' Hi! old man ', and he imitates Michel Simon. That came about the way you suggest.

CAHIERS — *One feels that the subject emerges only when the film is over. During the screening one thinks this is it, or that, but at the end one realises there was a real subject.*

GODARD — But that's cinema. Life arranges itself. One is never quite sure what one is going to do tomorrow, but at the end of the week one can say, after the event, ' I have lived ', like Musset's Camille. Then one realises one cannot trifle with the cinema either. You see someone in the street; out of ten passers-by there is one you look at more closely for one reason or another. If it's a girl, because she has eyes like so, a man because he has a particular air about him, and then you film their life. A subject will emerge which will be the person himself, his idea of the world, and the world created by this idea of it, the overall idea which this conjures. In the preface to one of his books, Antonioni says precisely this.

CAHIERS — *One feels that Pierrot takes place in two periods. In the first, Karina and Belmondo make their way to the Côte d'Azur, no cinema, because this is their life; and then, on arrival, they met a director and told him their story, and he made them begin all over again.*

GODARD — To a certain extent, yes, because the whole last part was invented on the spot, unlike the beginning which was planned. It is a kind of happening, but one that was controlled and dominated. This said, it is a completely spontaneous film. I have never been so worried as I was two days before shooting began. I had nothing, nothing at all. Oh well, I had the book. And a certain number of locations. I knew it would take place by the sea. The whole thing was shot, let's say like in the days of Mack Sennett. Maybe I am growing more and more apart from one section of current film-making. Watching old films, one never gets the impression that they were bored working, probably because the cinema was something new in those days, whereas today people tend to look on it as very old. They say ' I saw an old Chaplin film, an old Griffith film ', whereas no one says ' I read an old Stendhal, an old

Madame de La Fayette '.

*

CAHIERS — *Early films tell us a good deal about the period in which they were made. This is no longer true of 75% of current productions. In* Pierrot le Fou, *do contemporary life and the fact that Belmondo is writing his journal give the film its real dimension?*

GODARD — Anna represents the active life and Belmondo the contemplative. This is by way of contrasting them. As they are never analysed, there are no analytical scenes or dialogue. I wanted, indirectly through the journal, to give the feeling of reflection.

CAHIERS — *Your characters allow themselves to be guided by events.*

GODARD — They are abandoned to their own devices. They are inside both their adventure and themselves.

CAHIERS — *The only real act Belmondo accomplishes is when he tries to extinguish the fuse.*

Godard — If he had put it out, he would have become different afterwards. He is like Piccoli in *Le Mépris*.

CAHIERS — *The adventure is sufficiently total for one not to be able to know what comes next.*

GODARD — This is because it is a film about the adventure rather than about the adventurers. A film about adventurers is Anthony Mann's *The Far Country,* where you think about the adventure because they are adventurers : whereas in *Pierrot le Fou,* one thinks it is about adventurers because it describes an adventure. Anyway it is difficult to separate one from the other. We know from Sartre that the free choice which the individual himself makes is mingled with what is usually his destiny.

CAHIERS — *Even more than in* Le Mépris, *the poetic presence of the sea . . .*

GODARD — This was deliberate, much more so than in *Le Mépris*. This is the theme.

CAHIERS — *Exactly as if the gods were in the sea.*

GODARD — No, nature; the presence of nature, which is neither romantic nor tragic.

CAHIERS — *Adventure seems to have vanished today, to be*

8

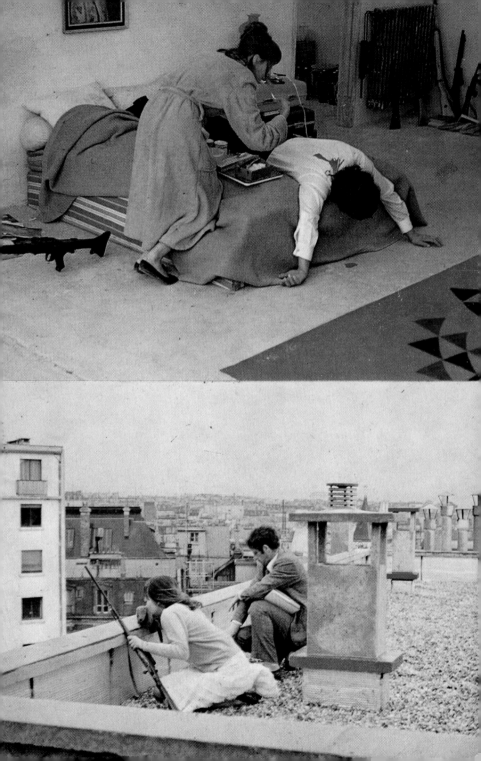

no longer welcome; hence the element of provocation now in adventure and in Pierrot le Fou.

GODARD — People pigeon-hole adventure. ' We're off on holiday ', they say, ' the adventure will begin as soon as we are at the seaside '. They don't think of themselves as living the adventure when they buy their train tickets, whereas in the film everything is on the same level : buying train tickets is as exciting as swimming in the sea.

CAHIERS — *Do you feel that all your films, irrespective of the way they are handled, are about the spirit of adventure?*

GODARD — Certainly. The important thing is to be aware one exists. For three-quarters of the time during the day one forgets this truth, which surges up again as you look at houses or a red light, and you have the sensation of existing in that moment. This was how Sartre began writing his novels. *La Nausée,* of course, was written during the great period when Simenon was publishing *Touristes de Bananes, Les Suicidés.* To me there is nothing very new about the idea, which is really a very classical one.

CAHIERS — Pierrot *is both classical — no trickery with montage — and modern, by virtue of its narrative.*

GODARD — What is modern by virtue of its narrative? I prefer to say its greater freedom. By comparison with my previous film, one gets an immediate response. Although I ask myself fewer and fewer questions now, one still remains : isn't no longer asking questions a serious thing? The thing that reassures me is that the Russians at the time of *October* and *Enthusiasm* didn't ask themselves questions. They didn't ask themselves what cinema should be. They didn't wonder if they should take up where the German cinema left off or repudiate films like *L'Assassinat du Duc de Guise.* No, there was a more natural way of asking questions. This is what one feels with Picasso. Posing problems is not a critical attitude but a natural function. When a motorist deals with traffic problems, one simply says he is driving; and Picasso that he paints.

*

CAHIERS — *For the majority of spectators, cinema exists only in terms of the Hollywood structures which have become*

13

convention, whereas all the great films are free in their inspiration.

GODARD — The great traditional cinema means Visconti as opposed to Fellini or Rossellini. It is a way of selecting certain scenes rather than others. The Bible is also a traditional book since it effects a choice in what it describes. If I were ever to film the life of Christ, I would film the scenes which are left out of the Bible. In *Senso,* which I quite like, it was the scenes which Visconti concealed that I wanted to see. Each time I wanted to know what Farley Granger said to Alida Valli, bang! — a fade out. *Pierrot le Fou,* from this standpoint, is the antithesis of *Senso :* the moments you do not see in *Senso* are shown in *Pierrot.*

CAHIERS — *Perhaps the beauty of the film springs from the fact that one senses this liberty more.*

GODARD — The trouble with the cinema is that it imposes a certain length of film. If my films reveal some feeling of freedom it is because I never think about length. I never know if what I am shooting will run twenty minutes or twice that, but it usually turns out that the result fits the commercial norm. I never have any time scheme. I shoot what I need, stopping when I think I have it all, continuing when I think there is more. This is full length dependent only on itself.

CAHIERS — *In a classical film, one would query the thriller framework.*

GODARD — On the narrative level, classical films can no longer rival even *Série Noire* thrillers, not to mention born storytellers like Giono who can hold you in suspense for days on end. The Americans are good at story-telling, the French are not. Flaubert and Proust can't tell stories. They do something else. So does the cinema, though starting from their point of arrival, from a totality. Any great modern film which is successful is so because of a misunderstanding. Audiences like *Psycho* because they think Hitchcock is telling them a story. *Vertigo* baffles them for the same reason.

*

CAHIERS — *With* Pierrot le Fou, *one feels one is watching the birth of cinema.*

GODARD — I felt this with Rossellini's film about steel, because it captured life at source. Television, in theory, should have the same effect. Thanks to the cultural alibi, there is no such thing as noble or plebeian subjects. Everything is possible on television. Very different from the cinema, where it would be impossible to film the building of the Boulevard Haussmann because to a distributor this isn't a noble subject.

CAHIERS — *Why do you think certain scenes are filmed rather than others? Does this choice define liberty or lead to convention?*

GODARD — The problem which has long preoccupied me, but which I don't worry about while shooting, is : why do one shot rather than another? Take a story for example. A character enters a room — one shot. He sits down — another shot. He lights a cigarette, etc. If, instead of treating it this way, one . . . would the film be better or less good?

What is it ultimately that makes one run a shot on or change to another? A director like Delbert Mann probably doesn't think this way. He follows a pattern. Shot — the character speaks; reverse angle, someone answers. Maybe this is why *Pierrot le Fou* is not a film, but an attempt at film.

CAHIERS — *And what Fuller says at the beginning?*

GODARD — I had wanted to say it for a long time. I asked him to. But it was Fuller himself who found the word ' emotion '. The comparison between film and a commando operation is from every point of view — financial, economic, artistic — a perfect image, a perfect symbol for a film in its totality.

CAHIERS — *Who is the enemy?*

GODARD — There are two things to consider. On the one hand the enemy who harries you; on the other, the goal to be reached, where the enemy may be. The goal to be reached is the film, but once it is finished one realises it was only a passage, a path to the goal. What I mean is that when the war is won, life continues. And maybe the film really begins then.

CAHIERS — *Isn't this sort of liberty in the cinema rather frightening?*

GODARD — No more than crossing a road either using a crossing or not. *Pierrot* seems to me both free and confined at the same time. What worries me most about this apparent liberty is something else. I read something by Borges where he spoke of a man who wanted to create a world. So he created houses, provinces, valleys, rivers, tools, fish, lovers, and then at the end of his life he notices that this 'patient labyrinth is none other than his own portrait'. I had this same feeling in the middle of *Pierrot*.

CAHIERS — *Why the quotation about Velasquez?*

GODARD — This is the theme. Its definition. Velasquez at the end of his life no longer painted precise forms, he painted what lay between the precise forms, and this is restated by Belmondo when he imitates Michel Simon : one should not describe people, but what lies between them.

CAHIERS — *If* Pierrot le Fou *is an instinctive film, one might wonder why there are connections with life and actuality.*

GODARD — It is inevitable, since making *Pierrot le Fou* consisted of living through an event. An event is made up of other events which one eventually discovers. In general, I repeat, making a film is an adventure comparable to that of an army advancing through a country and living off the inhabitants. So one is led to talk about these inhabitants. That is what actuality is : it is both what one calls actuality in the cinematic and journalistic sense, and casual encounter; what one reads, conversations, the business of living, in other words.

CAHIERS — *Each time actuality crops up in the film, one has the impression that there is a rupture in mood.*

GODARD — When, for instance?

CAHIERS — *The Vietnam war references . . .*

GODARD — I don't think so. In a world of violence, it is violence that controls the way things evolve. Anna and Belmondo meet some American tourists, and they know how to amuse them. They play the game. If they had met Russian or Spanish tourists, they would probably have acted differently. Of course, it was I who chose to have American tourists rather than any other. But in any case it suited the improvised theatre aspect. Someone coming back from China told me this is how it happens : suddenly, in a market-place, five people come along; one plays the American imperialist, and so on. Just like children playing cops and robbers. My inclusion of a newsreel about Vietnam after that was pure logic : it was to show Belmondo that they were playing a game, but that nevertheless the matter of their game pre-existed.

CAHIERS — *Conversely, would you consider filming a political subject with individual repercussions?*

GODARD — A purely political subject is difficult to do. For politics, you need insight into the points of view of four or five different people, and at the same time have a broad overall grasp. Politics involves both past and present. When you read Churchill's memoirs, you understand very clearly what is happening today. You think, so that is what he was thinking when he took part in such and such a conference; but you only learn this twenty years later. It is more difficult in the cinema : you have no time since you are dealing with the present. What would interest me is the life of a student, the story of *Clarté,* for instance. But a film about the life of an editor of *Clarté* would have been possible two years ago. Now it's too late, or too soon. It should have been done at the time, since the situation made it possible, with a broad outline scenario, and working along *cinéma-vérité* lines subject to direction and structural organisation.

CAHIERS — *It is often said that dragging politics like this into a story such as the Anna-Belmondo adventure is dilettantism.*

GODARD — The answer to that is simply : you can read *Le Monde* seriously or as a dilettante. Either way, the fact is that you do read it, and that is part of life. In the cinema, however, one shouldn't, if one is in a room, simply open the window and film what is going on outside. The discontented see this as a rupture in unity, but for all that fail to see where the unity lies. One may feel that in *Pierrot* the unity is purely emotional, and point out that something does not fit this emotional unity; but simply to say that politics have no right to be there is pointless, since they are part of the emotional unity. Here we come back to the old classification by genres: a film is poetic, psychological, tragic, but it is not allowed simply to be a film. Naturally if I were to make a film about the Dreyfus case, you would see very little about the case and a good deal about people and their personal relationships. Another fascinating thing to do now would be the life of a shorthand-typist at Auschwitz (Mikhail Romm has made a documentary compilation along these lines called *Ordinary Fascism*). But a film about a shorthand-typist at Auschwitz would be hated by everybody. The so-called left wing has always been the first to criticise the real left wing film-makers, both Pasolini and Rossellini in Italy, Dovzhenko and Eisenstein in Russia. One can only talk about the milieu one knows at first; later, with age and experience, this milieu opens out. It is very curious that in France there have never been any films about the Resistance. The Italians, of course, deal with the problem of the Resistance and the Liberation in political terms because they had experienced them in a much more obvious way, and Fascism had affected Italy more than France. Yet from an emotional point of view, the lives of the generation before our own were completely disrupted by the war. Even now they are still living the pre-war days and have not emerged into the post-war period. But no films about this either. No film about the adventures of the Ponchardier brothers, the real Frank and Jesse James of the Resistance. In America or Russia there would have been twenty films about Moulin, the Maquis of Glières, and so on. In France, one film did try to evoke the ambiance of 1944, Dewever's *Les Honneurs de la Guerre*. It was all but banned. As soon as a film comes along which is more or less honest, a climate, of suspicion and disparagement spring up.

*

CAHIERS — *What about colour in* Pierrot le Fou? *For instance, the coloured reflections on the windscreen of the car . . .*

GODARD — When you drive in Paris at night, what do you see? Red, green, yellow lights. I wanted to show these elements but without necessarily placing them as they are in reality. Rather as they remain in the memory — splashes of red and green, flashes of yellow passing by. I wanted to recreate a sensation through the elements which constitute it.

CAHIERS — *This is the hand of the painter again . . .*

GODARD — But I think one can go much further in this

18

direction — without, however, repeating what Butor did in literature. That is too easy to achieve in the cinema. Writers have always wanted to use the cinema as a blank page : to arrange all the elements and to let the mind circulate from one to the other. But this is not easy to do in the cinema. Contrary to what Belmondo says in *Pierrot*, Joyce is of no interest to the cinema. In any case the silent cinema went just as far. We have lost a considerable part of the silent cinema's discoveries, and are only now beginning to rediscover them because we are reverting to simplicity, and because the influence of the sound cinema as it was practised is beginning to disappear. The great silent cinema never meant the application of a certain style to a certain event. In my opinion the cinema should be more poetic — and poetic in a broader sense, while poetry itself should be opened out.

CAHIERS — *One must deal with anything and everything.*

GODARD — Two or three years ago I felt that everything had been done, that there was nothing left to do today. I couldn't see anything to do that hadn't been done already. *Ivan the Terrible* had been made, and *Our Daily Bread.* Make films about the people, they said; but *The Crowd* had already been made, so why remake it? I was, in a word, pessimistic. After *Pierrot,* I no longer feel this. Yes. One must film everything — talk about everything. Everything remains to be done.

(*Cahiers du Cinéma* No. 171, October 1965. Extracts from an interview by Jean-Louis Comolli, Michael Delahaye, Jean-André Fieschi and Gérard Guégan.)

CREDITS :

Script by	Jean-Luc Godard based on the novel *Obsession* by Lionel White
Directed by	Jean-Luc Godard
Produced by	Georges de Beauregard
Production	Rome-Paris Films (Paris)/Dino de Laurentiis Cinematographica (Rome)
Director of photography	Raoul Coutard
Production manager	René Demoulin
Music by	Antoine Duhamel
Songs ' Ma ligne de chance ' and ' Jamais je ne t'ai dit que je t'aimerai toujours ' by	Antoine Duhamel and Bassiak
Assistant directors	Philippe Fourastié and Jean-Pierre Léaud
Sound	René Levert
Art director	Pierre Guffroy
Camera operator	Georges Liron
Editor	Françoise Collin
Time	110 minutes
Process	Eastman Colour
Shot during	June-July 1965 on location in Paris and the South of France
First shown	29th August 1965 at the Venice Film Festival

CAST :

Ferdinand	Jean-Paul Belmondo
Marianne	Anna Karina
Marianne's brother, Fred	Dirk Sanders
Devos	Raymond Devos
Ferdinand's wife	Graziella Galvani
Gangsters	Roger Dutoit and Hans Meyer
The Midget	Jimmy Karoubi
Mme. Staquet	Christa Nell
Princess Aicha Abidir	Herself
Samuel Fuller	Himself
The Sailor	Alexis Poliakoff
Political exile from Santo Domingo	Lazlo Szabo
Young man in cinema	Jean-Pierre Léaud
Others	Pascal Aubier, Pierre Hanin

PIERROT LE FOU

Titles: on a black screen appear a number of red letter A's seemingly placed at random. The letters of the alphabet, in order, appear at brief intervals, all red, except for the line of the main title which is blue. Harsh, sinister music is heard. Finally, the full titles, in blue, can be read:

JEAN-PAUL BELMONDO
ET
ANNA KARINA
DANS
PIERROT LE FOU
UN FILM DE
JEAN-LUC GODARD

FERDINAND'S *voice is heard before the title is complete, and continues over the first four shots.*
Medium close-up of a young girl, facing the camera, playing tennis.
Long-shot from the edge of the tennis court. Two girls are knocking-up. It is a beautiful summer day. Medium shot of FERDINAND, *who is browsing among some bookstands outside a bookstore, called Les Meilleurs Des Mondes. He is carrying a large comic book under his arm.*
A wide river at dusk, with the lights of the city reflecting on the water; behind the buildings in the distance, the sky is deep red from the setting sun.
FERDINAND *off*: 'After he had reached the age of fifty, Velasquez no longer painted anything concrete and precise. He drifted through the material world, penetrating it, as the air and the dusk. In the shimmering of the shadows, he caught unawares the nuances of colour which he transformed into the invisible heart of his symphony of silence . . . His only experience of the world was those mysterious copulations which united the forms and tones with a secret but inevitable

movement, which no convulsion or cataclysm could ever interrupt or impede. Space reigned supreme . . . It was as if some tenuous radiation gliding over the surfaces, imbued itself of their visible emanations, modelling them and endowing them with form, carrying elsewhere a perfume, like an echo, which would thus be dispersed like an imponderable dusk, over all the surrounding planes . . .'

FERDINAND *is in his bath reading from a paperback history of art,* a cigarette arrogantly dangling from his lips.*

FERDINAND : 'The world he lived in was sad. A degenerate king, inbred infantas, idiots, dwarfs, cripples, deformed clowns clothed as princes, whose only job was to laugh at themselves and amuse those lifeless outlaws who were trapped by etiquette, conspiracy, lies, and inextricably bound to the confessional by guilt. Outside the gates, the Auto-da-fé, and silence . . .'

FERDINAND *turns to someone off screen.*

FERDINAND : What about that, my little girl!

His young DAUGHTER, *aged about five, crosses to the bath and sits next to him, patiently listening as he pontificates from the bathtub. She places her hand obediently on the edge of the bath.*

FERDINAND : 'A spirit of nostalgia prevailed. But we see none of the ugliness or sadness or any of the signs of gloom and cruelty of this crippled infancy. Velasquez is the painter of the evening, of the plains, of the silence, even when he paints in broad daylight, even when he paints in a closed room, even while hunting and war thrashes around him. Spanish painters never went outside except at those times in the day when the air was radiant, when everything was burnished by the sun. They discoursed only with the evening . . .'

FERDINAND: Don't you think that's beautiful, my little Poppet?

He turns to his DAUGHTER *who is listening with awe.*

A WOMAN *off* : You're mad to read them things like that!

The WOMAN *crosses the screen towards the child. We*

---

* Elie Faure's *Histoire de L'Art,* L'Art Moderne I. Page 167. Editions le Livre de Poche.

see nothing except her skirt as she drags the child away.
FERDINAND *looks disgusted.*
FERDINAND : Go on! Go and get laid . . . And why hasn't
Odile put them to bed, anyway!
The little GIRL *runs out from the bathroom into the bedroom, followed by her* MOTHER, *who stops and examines
her make-up in the tall mirror.*
WOMAN : Because *Monsieur* allowed them to go to the cinema
for the third time this week.
*FERDINAND emerges from the bathroom wearing a bath-
robe, and a long towel slung around his neck. He looks
at himself in the mirror and then cleans his feet with the
towel, nearly falling over in the process.*
FERDINAND : For the third time this week! They must be
playing *Johnny Guitar* down there; it's good she's getting the
right education. We're living in a world of idiots too much.
*Medium shot of their bedroom. He sits down on the
edge of the double bed, facing the camera, with his back
to his* WIFE *who sits on the other side. He is fed up. He
picks up the book he was reading, which he had put
down on the bedside table.*
WIFE : Come on! Hurry up! Frank and Paola will be here
any minute.
FERDINAND : I'm not going. No, I'm not going. That's final!
I'll stay here with the kids.
WIFE : Oh no, listen . . . Frank told me he would bring his
niece along to baby-sit until we got back. She's a student.
FERDINAND : Since when did he have a niece? I know him too
well. She must be a call-girl.
The WIFE *gets up and flings a towel at him, which
wraps round his face.*
FERDINAND : I'm not going!
WIFE : You'll do what I tell you. My father's going to intro-
duce you to the Managing Director of Standard Oil.
FERDINAND : And I'll bring legal action against the Television
Company for giving me the sack.
WIFE : Really . . . when we get some work for you, you'll be
decent enough to accept it. Allez! Basta!
She rudely grabs the book out of his hand. He turns

*round as if to play the insolent child and cheekily picks
up a pair of her panties on the bed.*

FERDINAND : Aren't you wearing anything under your skirt?
Aren't you wearing a petticoat?

WIFE : No, I'm wearing my new invisible panty-girdle which
you can't see.

*She hands him a woman's magazine, and shows him the
advert for her new girdle. He picks it up and starts to
read aloud. As he does so we see the page of the
magazine in close-up. The camera pans down and pans
up again as he reads. His last words overlap onto the
next image, emphasising their absurdity.*

FERDINAND *off* : Under my new knickers . . . ' SCANDALE '
. . . youthful contours. There was the Greek Civilisation, there
was the Renaissance, and now we are entering the Age of the
Arse.

WIFE : Come on, I'll show you . . .

FERDINAND : She adores children !

*Medium shot of the WIFE leading her two small
children down the hall past the visitors who have arrived.
MARIANNE is sitting on the right, very demure and innocent, playing with a woolly toy dog, a dachshund,
in her lap. She gets up and follows the WIFE and the
children. The camera pans with her. She is wearing a
navy blue blazer over a white blouse, and has her hair
tied back into bunches. As we follow them along the
hall, FERDINAND comes out of the bedroom straightening
his tie. He has just put on a clean white shirt.*

WIFE *to* MARIANNE : And if you need us for anything you can
call us at . . . *She asks* FRANK. What's the number?

FRANK : 225-70-01.

WIFE *to* FERDINAND : Ah! Here's Frank's niece.

*She introduces her husband to MARIANNE. They shake
hands with a touch of familiarity, without really stopping, lingering, as their hands meet just long enough to
look into each other's eyes.*

FERDINAND : Good evening . . .

*MARIANNE goes off with the WIFE and the camera pans
with FERDINAND until he greets FRANK : Salut! Suddenly*

26

his behaviour is transformed. He seems to be triggered off by some inner event. He abandons his lethargy as he grabs his jacket, picks up some cigarettes off a side table, and jokes with FRANK *about the telephone.*

FERDINAND : 225 — you can't say Balzac? You don't know Balzac? Read César Birotteau — and the three chords of the Fifth Symphony which thundered in his poor head!

FRANK : What's he on tonight?

FERDINAND : Come on, let's go, allons-y, alonzo . . .

He flings open the door and lurches out into the night as if hell bent on some adventure, as if the prospect of it has suddenly turned him on, transformed his despair into excitement . . . FRANK *hastily follows, pulling his wife with him.*

Long-shot of the Champs Elysées at night, with the floodlit Arc de Triomphe dominating the image. The opening chords of Beethoven's Fifth Symphony accompanies FERDINAND'S *voice off, as he starts to describe the scenes that follow, each one parodying the colour and style of the commercials shown in French cinemas, advertising cosmetics, cars, chocolates, etc. . . .*

FERDINAND *off* : Chapter Two. A surprise-party. *In English* : at the home of *Monsieur* and *Madame* Expresso, whose daughter is my wife.

Image in red only: several guests at the party standing elegantly poised, drinks in hand, boringly churning out their bourgeois platitudes.

MALE GUEST : An Alfa-Romeo does the first kilometre from start in 34 seconds — fantastic braking power — four discs, marvellously comfortable, and, of course, what road-holding! . . . Cruises exceptionally well, is sure, fast, pleasant to drive, sensitive and well balanced.

FEMALE GUEST : Keeping fresh is easy. Lava soap, Eau de Cologne, scented perfume. To avoid all smell of perspiration I use Printil after washing and I'm absolutely perfect for the rest of the day. Printil comes in an atomiser, so fresh; or spray, stick or bottle.

MALE GUEST : But the Oldsmobile Rocket 88 offers so much more, its design is handsome and strong, its line powerful yet sober, a rare elegance which proves that beauty is not incompatible with high performance.

FERDINAND *walks slowly from right to left with a glass in his hand. As he reaches the left side of the screen, the camera cuts to a similar shot with different guests, in normal full colour. He stops between a girl who is sitting down on his right, and a tough-looking American on his left, drinking whisky and looking very bored.* FERDINAND *turns to the man and starts a conversation. He cannot understand French so refers the questions to the girl, who interprets the conversation in French and English.*

FERDINAND : You appear to be lonely . . .

AMERICAN *to the* GIRL *in English* : What did he say?

GIRL *in English* : You're alone? *She turns to* FERDINAND. He's an American and can't speak French.

FERDINAND : What's his name, and what does he do?

GIRL *in English* : Who are you? What are you doing?

AMERICAN *in English* : I'm an American film director. My name is Samuel Fuller. I'm here to make a film in Paris : *Flowers of Evil.*

GIRL : It's Samuel Fuller, an American. He's a film director, here to make *Fleurs du Mal.*

FERDINAND : Baudelaire. That's great. *He turns again to* FULLER. I've always wanted to know exactly what the cinema is.

GIRL *in English* : He says he wants to know exactly what is movies.

AMERICAN *in English* : The film is like a battleground.

GIRL : The film is like a battleground.

AMERICAN *in English* : Yes . . . Love.

GIRL : Love.

AMERICAN *in English* : Hate.

GIRL : Hate.

AMERICAN *in English* : Action.

GIRL : Action.

AMERICAN *in English* : Violence.

GIRL : Violence.

AMERICAN *in English* : Death.

GIRL : And Death.

AMERICAN *in English* : In one word . . . Emotion.
GIRL : In one word . . . Emotion.
FERDINAND *looking into his glass, taking a huge gulp and throwing back his head* : . . Ah ! . .

A bright yellow image: a young man is talking to FERDINAND'S WIFE; *he stops and kisses her just as* FERDINAND *passes by.* FERDINAND *stops, pauses and watches them kiss. He walks off the screen to the left, unconcerned.*
Blue image: a similar couple, talking and drinking.

FEMALE GUEST : My hairdo, light and soft, stayed in place all day thanks to Elnett Satin Spray. With brushing, the lacquer disappears, as if it never existed. My hair is like strands of golden silk, shining and clean . . .

As previous images but in normal colour, a couple is seen drinking and talking. The man is in a dinner jacket, and the girl is wearing a topless dress. Both her partner and FERDINAND, *who is walking past, seem unaffected by the sight of her naked breasts.* FERDINAND *is walking slowly from right to left as before. The girl is talking.*

FEMALE GUEST : Women must stop wearing transparent housecoats and romantic nightdresses. In daylight or any bright light, lingerie looses all its magic and becomes indecent. (*Still on page 10*)

Blue image: a couple is sitting at both sides of a table, beneath a forbidding French tapestry on the wall. As FERDINAND *passes, the man leans over and lights the girl's cigarette. As he clicks the lighter shut the coloured filter changes from blue to green.* FERDINAND *goes off screen to the left, after commenting* . . .

FERDINAND : Olympio's Sadness.

Blue image: FERDINAND *meets* FRANK *and a* WOMAN. *He sits down next to* FRANK, *tired and bored.* (*Still on page 9*)

FERDINAND *to* FRANK : Give me the keys of the Lincoln.
FRANK : Aren't you staying?
FERDINAND : No . . . I'm worn out. I've a mechanism for seeing, called eyes, for listening, called ears, for speaking,

33

called mouth. I've got a feeling they're all going their separate ways . . . There's no co-ordination. One should feel they're united. I feel they are deranged.

WOMAN : You talk too much! I'm tired just listening to you.

FERDINAND : Yes, it's true . . . I do talk too much. Lonely people always talk too much. I'll wait for you at the house.

He stands up and FRANK *hands him the keys.*

FERDINAND *pushes his way violently through a group of guests to reach a table on which there is a huge iced cake. He grabs a fistful of cake and flings it at the frightened guests who cower away from the ' madman' in their midst . . . As he throws the creamcake the image cuts to a firework exploding in the sky at night . . .*

FERDINAND *off:* Next Chapter :
> Despair
> Memory and Freedom
> Sorrow
> Hope
> The pursuit of time passed away
> Marianne Renoir

Interior of FERDINAND'S *apartment.* FERDINAND *enters on the left and closes the door. As he climbs over his children's miniature sports car, parked perilously in the middle of the hall, he notices something off screen to the right. Camera pans with him as he approaches stealthily and whispers to* MARIANNE. *She is asleep on a chair, resting her head against the bureau, beneath a drawing by Renoir. On her lap, open, is the huge comic book that* FERDINAND *had been carrying under his arm at the bookshop. He touches her gently to wake her.*

FERDINAND : Are you still here? . . .

MARIANNE *waking up:* I'm . . . sorry . . . I . . .

FERDINAND : It's too late for the Métro. How will you get home?

MARIANNE : I don't know . . . Are you on your own?

FERDINAND : Yes, I got bored so I came home.

MARIANNE : Is everything all right? You look awfully depressed.

FERDINAND : Well, some days are like that . . . everyone you meet is an imbecile. Then you look in a mirror and start wondering about yourself . . . Come on. I'll take you home.

As they are talking, there is a clap of thunder and the sound of torrential rain. She gets up and follows him from the apartment, carrying the big comic book under her arm.

Long-shot of fireworks exploding in the night sky. MARIANNE *is seen through the front windscreen of a car. It is night and the green and red reflected lights of a motorway zoom up and over the windscreen. The lights seem to start in the throat, flood through the face and fly off at a tangent into the sky. The image stays in medium close-up on* MARIANNE *as she talks with* FERDINAND, *who is driving, off screen on her right.*

MARIANNE : Frank lent you his car?

FERDINAND *off:* Yes . . . Why don't you like Americans?

MARIANNE : Yeah! . . . yeah! It's rather funny meeting each other again isn't it!

FERDINAND *off* : It must be four years.

MARIANNE : No, five and a half. It was October. Are you married?

FERDINAND *off*: Yes. I found myself a rich Italian girl. But she doesn't interest me very much.

MARIANNE : Why not get a divorce?

FERDINAND *off* : I wanted to, but I've become too lazy . . . desire . . . in desire, you once pointed out, there is life. I wanted desire, I was alive . . .*

MARIANNE : You still teach Spanish at St. Louis?

FERDINAND *off* : No. I work in Television. But I made a mess. And you?

MARIANNE : Me, nothing in particular.

FERDINAND *off* : You don't like talking about yourself?

MARIANNE : No.

FERDINAND *off* : A friend of mine saw you in London a couple of years ago. Do you still knock around with that American?

MARIANNE : No, it finished a long time ago.

---

* Translator's note : FERDINAND puns on the French word for desire ' envie ' and the phrase ' en vie ', in life — thus — j'avais envie, j'étais en vie '.

FERDINAND *off* : And Frank, have you known him long?

MARIANNE : No, not really . . . very casual.

FERDINAND *off* : Still mysterious.

MARIANNE : No, I just don't like talking about myself, as I told you.

On his suggestion of silence she leans forward and switches on the car radio, smiling at him mischieviously.

FERDINAND *off* : Okay . . . right . . . then silence.

A news bulletin cuts in gratingly with its latest facts from the Vietnam war.

RADIO : . . . garrison already decimated by the Vietcong, who lost 115 of their men . . . thus drawing to a close . . .

The camera remains on his face while she does most of the talking. From time to time, he looks round at her. He is smoking.

MARIANNE *off* : It's awful isn't it, it's so anonymous.

FERDINAND : What is?

MARIANNE *off* : They say 115 guerrillas, yet it doesn't mean anything, because we don't know anything about these men, who they are, whether they love a woman, or have children, if they prefer the cinema to the theatre. We know nothing. They just say . . . 115 dead. It's like photographs. They've always fascinated me. You see a still photograph of some man or other, with a caption underneath. He was a coward perhaps, or pretty smart. But at that precise instant when the photograph was taken, no one can say what he actually is, and what he was thinking exactly . . . about his wife maybe, or his mistress, his past, his future, or basket-ball . . . One never knows.

Close-up of MARIANNE. *As* FERDINAND *takes up the conversation, we see her reactions.*

FERDINAND : Yeah . . .that's life !

MARIANNE : Yes, what makes me sad is that life in novels is so very different. I'd like it to be the same, clear, logical, formal. But it's not like that at all.

FERDINAND : It is, much more than people believe.

MARIANNE : No, Pierrot.

FERDINAND : I'm not going to tell you again, my name is Ferdinand.

MARIANNE : Yes, but one can say . . . ' My friend Ferdinand '
. . . *she sings it to a musical phrase, laughing at her private
joke.*
FERDINAND : Yes, one only needs to want something,
Marianne . . .
MARIANNE, *music fades in as if she is going to sing ' Mon Ami
Ferdinand ' :* I want . . . I will do everything you want me to.
FERDINAND : Me too, Marianne.
MARIANNE : I'll put my hand on your knee.
FERDINAND : Me too, Marianne.
MARIANNE : I'll kiss you all over.
FERDINAND : Me too, Marianne.
> *Close-up of* MARIANNE, *her hair blowing in the wind. It
> is daylight. Music quietly fades away. Sadly, and pen-
> sively, she says . . .*
MARIANNE : We will see . . . in time.
> *Close-up of Renoir's painting ' Portrait of a Little Girl.'*
FERDINAND *off* : Marianne Renoir.
> *Interior of an apartment.* MARIANNE, *dressed in a blue
> towelling bathrobe, is in a sparsely furnished kitchen.
> The walls are white. Reproductions of paintings by
> Picasso, Renoir and Modigliani are pinned haphazardly
> to the walls, together with photographs from* Life *and*
> Paris-Match *magazines.* MARIANNE *is filling a red
> enamel pan with water from a hose pipe.*
> *Medium shot of* FERDINAND *as he wakes up in bed
> in the next room; he drags his head from the pillow with
> great effort, and lets out a horrible cry of anguish,
> perhaps mocking, perhaps in earnest.*
MARIANNE *off* : Okay, on your feet, you corpse!
> *Long-shot of the other room,* MARIANNE *enters from
> the patio roof and goes and pours the water from one
> pan into another. She opens the door of a fridge, look-
> ing over her shoulder anxiously all the time to the left.
> The camera pans with her as she moves left, passing a
> photograph of Tshombe and a Modigliani painting.
> She bends down at the side of a double bed on the
> left of the room and, as she takes a breakfast tray from
> the bed, we see for the first time the body of a man*

37

lying face downwards. A pair of scissors is embedded in his neck. His shirt is covered with blood. She picks up the tray, as if the body did not exist. (Still on page 11) She enters from the right into the next room, carrying the breakfast tray. She puts it on FERDINAND'S *knees as he sits up in the bed, resting his back against the white wall.*

FERDINAND : You see, I was right.

MARIANNE : What?

FERDINAND : You didn't believe me when I told you we would always love each other.

MARIANNE : No.

Music fades in and she starts to sing him a song by Bassiak. He sits up in bed eating his breakfast. She goes behind a screen and brings out a pink dress on a hanger. She ruffles his hair then rests her cheek on the door-jamb as she sings to him.

MARIANNE *singing* : I never told you that I would love you
    all my life,
    Oh my love;
    You never promised to adore me all
    your life;
    We never exchanged such promises,
    knowing me,
    Knowing you . . .
    We could never have known that we
    would ever fall in love :
    We were so unfaithful.
    And yet . . . and yet . . . very gently,
    without a word spoken between us,
    Little by little,
    A true emotion has crept into our
    bodies which enjoyed being together
    so much . . .

Close-up of MARIANNE *in another room looking at herself in the mirror as she sings and eats her toast; she licks her fingers, and picks up a jar of honey to take into* FERDINAND'S *room.*

MARIANNE *singing* : Then words of love came to our naked

MARIANNE *singing* :   lips,
Little by little,
Heaps of words mingled,
Very gently, with our kisses.
How many words of love?
I would never have believed that you
    would always please me,
Oh my love.
We never thought that we would be
    able to live together without ex-
    hausting each other.
We wake up every morning, still sur-
    prised to find ourselves so happy
    to be
In the same bed,
Wanting nothing more than each day
To be so glad to be together.
And yet . . . and yet . . . very gently,
    without a word spoken between us,
Little by little,
Our love has bound us together in
    spite of ourselves without even think-
    ing about it.
This feeling is stronger than all the
    words of love that are known
And unknown;
This feeling is so strong and so
    violent—
This feeling that we would never have
    believed possible.
You never promised to adore me all
    your life,
We certainly never exchanged any such
    promises, knowing me,
Knowing you . . .
Let us keep the knowledge that our love
    is a love . . .
That our love is a love
With no tomorrow.

Close-up of MARIANNE *against a white wall, looking at* FERDINAND *in his bed.*
Close-up of FERDINAND, *his cigarette drooping from his mouth, as he looks sorrowfully at her, then sadly and very slowly, he turns away and looks down . . .*
Medium close-up of MARIANNE, *still singing, as she leans over* FERDINAND *and takes the cigarette from his lips, kisses him and puts the cigarette back. Long-shot of the kitchen:* MARIANNE *closes the door of the fridge and goes to a small table in the corner against the wall. As she turns off the gas on the little calor-gas cooker, we see numerous rifles and guns stacked up in the corner. She takes the pan from the stove with a great flourish, casts an insolent glance at the dead body on the bed, and swirls through the door, dancing to the music, to be with* FERDINAND *again.*
She sits down on the bed across his feet, leaning against the wall, still singing . . . (Still on page 9) the camera tracks in fast to a close-up as the song ends.

FERDINAND *off*: Anyway, we'll know very well when we are dead . . . in sixty years, if we were always in love.

MARIANNE: But no . . . I'm sure that I love you . . . but you, I'm not so sure . . . I'm not at all sure.

FERDINAND: Yes, Marianne, yes.

MARIANNE: Good. I'm going to know it very well.
Close-up of Picasso's painting 'Pierrot au masque.' Montage of images from the postcard reproductions on the walls.

MARIANNE *off*: You know your wife was here this morning.

FERDINAND *off*: I couldn't care a damn!

MARIANNE *off*: And not only that.

FERDINAND *off*: I already told you, I really couldn't care a damn.
Close-up of two images of pistols on a table next to brightly coloured table lamps.

MARIANNE *off*: Marianne tells a story about . . .

FERDINAND *off*: Ferdinand.

MARIANNE *off*: A story . . .

FERDINAND *off*: Complicated.

MARIANNE *off* : I knew some people . . .

FERDINAND *off* : It's just like during the Algerian war.

MARIANNE *off* : I will explain everything to you.

FERDINAND *off* : Waking from a terrible dream . . .

Long-shot of FERDINAND, *now dressed, who goes into the large room and sees the body on the bed, obviously for the first time. He does not seem too surprised. He picks up one of the guns and puts it down again, as he surveys the room and its objects. He sits down on the bed next to the body, as* MARIANNE *comes in from the other room, now wearing the pink frilly dress she had taken from behind the screen earlier. They sit on the bed on both sides of the body, accompanied by ominous music. The letters OASIS on the wall, OAS in red, IS in blue.* MARIANNE *starts to empty the back trouser pockets on the corpse. She flings out the contents onto the floor, exasperated by not finding what she is looking for. A noise outside startles them both.* MARIANNE *leaps up and pushes* FERDINAND *back as he begins to rise. She flings open the fridge door and throws him a bottle of whisky which he catches. She hides down behind the fridge door as camera pans right and picks up* FRANK *entering from the outside. Their voices off, almost drowned by the music . . .*

FERDINAND *off* : Frank had the keys?

MARIANNE *off* : I'll explain everything to you.

FERDINAND *off* : You were lovers?

MARIANNE *off* : I'll explain everything to you.

FERDINAND *off* : Did he make love to you?

MARIANNE *off* : I'll explain everything to you.

Long-shot as FRANK *goes past the fridge, looks unemotionally at the body on the bed and goes through to the next room, and then out to the patio roof. He puts on his jacket, which he was carrying slung over one shoulder. As he comes back into the apartment,* FERDINAND *slips by behind him.* FRANK *and* MARIANNE *come out seconds later, and* FRANK *has his arms round her; she is laughing and flirting with him. They obviously know each other very well. She is again carry-*

*ing the large comic book under her arm. As they enter
the large room of the apartment again from the patio,*
FRANK *attempts to kiss* MARIANNE, *passionately. She
manages to signal to* FERDINAND *over* FRANK'S *shoulder
as she gently pushes him down on the bed as if
encouraging his passion. But then she opens the book
to read to him and he is obviously bewildered. To*
FRANK'S *amazement* FERDINAND *arrives from the door
on the left and, without a word, walks calmly past the
end of the bed circling round ominously.* FRANK *remains
seated.*

FERDINAND *goes behind* MARIANNE *who is still standing
with the open book in her hands.* FERDINAND *takes it
from her, carefully putting the whisky bottle into her
hands, which* FRANK *has still not noticed.* MARIANNE,
*smiling weakly and obviously more than a little worried,
creeps up stealthily behind* FRANK, *raises the bottle over
her head and crashes it down on* FRANK'S *skull. The
bottle smashes into pieces and* FRANK *collapses. He is
dragged out of the room by* FERDINAND. *Their voices off,
continue a dialogue of phrases, as short and as irrational
as the cutting of the next sequence. The time sequence in
the following montage has been abandoned and the
images are mostly too short to make much sense of. They
convey the confusion and excitement as* MARIANNE *and*
FERDINAND *escape in a car, just as two unidentified men
are seen arriving at the apartment in pursuit. One of
them is tall and wearing a light grey suit; the other is a
midget. The action is accompanied by the following
erratic dialogue.*

MARIANNE *off* : A story
FERDINAND *off* : Complicated
MARIANNE *off* : . . . leave very quickly
FERDINAND *off* : . . . waking from a bad dream
MARIANNE *off* : I knew some people
FERDINAND *off* : Politics
MARIANNE *off* : An Organisation
FERDINAND *off* : Go away
MARIANNE *off* : Gun-running

FERDINAND *off* : In silence . . . in silence . . . in silence
MARIANNE *off* : It's me, Marianne
FERDINAND *off* : He kissed you
MARIANNE *off* : A story
FERDINAND *off* : Complicated
MARIANNE *off* : I knew some people
FERDINAND *off* : You were lovers
MARIANNE *off* : Using my apartment
FERDINAND *off* : It was like during the Algerian War
MARIANNE *off* : I have a brother
FERDINAND *off* : Waking from a bad dream
MARIANNE *off* : Leave in a hurry . . . leave in a hurry . . .
leave in a hurry
FERDINAND *off* : Reply
MARIANNE *off* : Bored to death
FERDINAND *off* : Argument
MARIANNE *off* : Garage
FERDINAND *off* : Who is it?
MARIANNE *off* : In the Midi
FERDINAND *off* : Getting away
MARIANNE *off* : No money
FERDINAND *off* : In any case, it was the right moment to get
away from this stinking lousy world.
MARIANNE *off* : We left Paris by a one way street.
FERDINAND *off* : Recognising two of her own . . . the Statue
of Liberty gave us a friendly wave . . .

MARIANNE *runs out onto the patio roof and looks over
the edge into the street below, dashes frantically back
into the room where* FERDINAND *is still dragging* FRANK'S
body past the fridge.
*She has picked up the comic book again, and is carrying
a cardigan.*
She takes a rifle and rushes out onto the roof again.
In a long-shot from above, FERDINAND *jumps into a little
red car as it is moving away.*
He is holding the gun MARIANNE *had taken from the flat.*
*The two of them leaving the apartment and running
onto the patio roof.*
Travelling shot from inside the car as it approaches

and goes under a red and white construction barrier along the edge of the Seine.

The two of them rushing from the apartment again. Seen from the roof, the tall man and the midget running across a car park between the cars.

MARIANNE *and* FERDINAND *leaning over the balustrade of the patio looking down towards the cars below.* (*Still on page 11*)

FERDINAND *climbs down a drainpipe. As he jumps from the bottom of the drainpipe, he trips and falls, and drops the gun. He picks himself up and turns round to help* MARIANNE *to jump off after him.*

He catches her as she falls.

FERDINAND *jumps into the moving red car.*

The red car on a motorway seen speeding away from the camera.

The same red car in the car park.

MARIANNE *is getting into it on the driver's side and starts to drive it away.*

Red car on motorway coming towards the camera. Travelling shot along the bank of the Seine, with the Statue of Liberty at the end of the quay on the Isle de Paris . . . The car draws into a garage and stops in front of the petrol pumps. MARIANNE *leans out of the window and yells at the attendant.* FERDINAND *gets out of the car and also speaks to the attendant.*

FERDINAND : Put a tiger in the tank!

ATTENDANT : We don't sell tigers here.

FERDINAND : Well, in that case, fill her up and shut your mouth, my friend!

In medium close-up through one of the side windows we see them whispering, plotting . . .

MARIANNE : If it's me, he won't be so suspicious.

She gets out of the car, goes to the front and lifts up the bonnet. The attendant goes to FERDINAND *for the money.*

ATTENDANT : That's forty new francs.

FERDINAND : Oil and water too, old friend!

The attendant goes to the front of the car and leans under the bonnet to get at the engine. MARIANNE *slams*

44

*the bonnet down on his head and he crumples up un-
conscious.*

*Same scene from another angle. She beckons to
FERDINAND to come and help her.*

MARIANNE : Help me, you fool !

FERDINAND *gets out and drags the body from under the
bonnet and dumps it on the ground.* MARIANNE *closes
the bonnet.* FERDINAND, *however, sees another attendant
coming their way.*

FERDINAND : Shit ! There's another of them !

MARIANNE : I've just remembered a gag in a Laurel and
Hardy movie. You get in the car.

MARIANNE *and the attendant face each other, as she
listens to his complaint.*

ATTENDANT : What's got into you, aren't you ashamed?
Haven't you got any money?

MARIANNE : No, *Monsieur,* we haven't got any money.

ATTENDANT : And so, you'll have to work to earn some
money won't you? Don't you want to work?

MARIANNE : No, *Monsieur,* we don't want to work.

ATTENDANT : All right then, what do you intend to do to
pay for the petrol?

MARIANNE *points to the sky and he looks upwards. As
he does so she biffs him in the stomach and he crumples
up. She runs back to the car.*

FERDINAND : Shit ! — there's another one !

She gets into the car as FERDINAND *goes and spars with
the attendant in a shadow boxing match, neither of
them seeming to connect.* MARIANNE *drives towards
them just as* FERDINAND *knocks the guy to the ground.
She nearly drives over his head.* FERDINAND *gets into the
car as the attendant picks himself up and runs off towards
his office shouting . . .*

ATTENDANT : Must call the police !

*Camera pans with the car as it leaves the garage court-
yard and pans up to the sign ' TOTAL.'*

FERDINAND *off* : Total.

Close-up of a pop-art type comic cartoon image.

MARIANNE *off* : It was an adventure film.

Close-up of Picasso's painting 'The Lovers.'
FERDINAND *off* : Diadem of Blood.
Close-up of another painting, perhaps by Rouault.
MARIANNE *off* : Total.
FERDINAND *off* : Tender is the night.
MARIANNE *off* : It was a love story. It was a love story.
FERDINAND *off* : Tender is the night.
MARIANNE *off* : It was a love story.
Inside the car at night, driving along a motorway, the lights rocketing up and over the windscreen as before. Close-up of FERDINAND.
MARIANNE *off* : I think the best thing we can do is to find my brother.
FERDINAND : What precisely is his racket ?
MARIANNE *off* : Oh, things in Africa . . . Angola . . . Congo . . .
FERDINAND : I thought he was supposed to be a broadcaster for Monte Carlo Television.
MARIANNE *off* : Yes . . . that too.
FERDINAND : We've got to make a decision. Where are we going?
Close-up of MARIANNE.
MARIANNE : We said Nice . . . and after that perhaps Italy.
FERDINAND *off* : You know that twelve thousand francs aren't going to get us to Nice? We'd be better off abandoning the 404.
MARIANNE : Have you killed a man before, Pierrot?
FERDINAND : My name is Ferdinand. Why do you ask?
MARIANNE : Because it'll have a bad effect on you, you know . . .
Close-up of FERDINAND.
FERDINAND : I wonder what she told the police? Perhaps they haven't questioned her yet.
MARIANNE : Don't be a fool ! She'll have said everything nasty about you she could think of.
FERDINAND : She's right. In any case, I'm pretty sorry for her.
MARIANNE : Sorry? Men like you are always sorry. But always too late.
Long-shot of the car drawing off the road onto a verge.

46

*When the headlights go out the only thing visible is the
indicator winking.*

*Close-up as they kiss each other tenderly and passion-
ately. Afterwards he turns the inside mirror round and
looks at himself in it.*

MARIANNE : What are you doing?

FERDINAND : I'm looking at myself.

MARIANNE : And what do you see?

FERDINAND : The face of a man who's about to throw himself
over a precipice at a hundred miles an hour.

*She moves the mirror and turns it so she can see her own
face in it.*

MARIANNE : Well, *I* can see the face of a woman who is in
love with a man who is just about to throw himself over a
precipice at a hundred miles an hour.

FERDINAND : So, kiss me then. *Music fades in.*

*Another long-shot of the car at the side of the road, the
indicator still winking.*

*Close-up of comic-strip cover for a crime novel. A girl
with a revolver pointing at the camera. The word
' RENDEZVOUS.'*

FERDINAND *off* : The following day. The following day.

Long-shot of the car driving along the road.

FERDINAND *off* : The following day. The following day.

MARIANNE *off* : We see the 404 . . .

FERDINAND *off* : . . . arriving in a little village in Central
France.

MARIANNE *off* : There's almost no petrol . . .

FERDINAND *off* : . . . in the car.

MARIANNE *off* : Marianne

FERDINAND *off* : . . . and Ferdinand

MARIANNE *off* : . . . stop in front of a Bar.

*Long-shot from above, the car arrives outside a small
village Bar. They leave the car and go inside.*

MARIANNE *off* : They order something . . .

FERDINAND *off* : . . . wondering . . .

MARIANNE *off* : . . . how they'll pay for it.

*Medium shot of the interior of the café. While ordering
they listen anxiously to a transistor radio. They hold it*

close to their ears so that no one else will hear.
Same shot from the front. (Still on page 12)
MARIANNE *off* : The police are broadcasting their descriptions on the radio.
FERDINAND *off* : People look at them suspiciously.
MARIANNE *off* : The police des . . .
FERDINAND *off* : People . . .
MARIANNE *off* : The police des . . .
FERDINAND *off* : People . . .
MARIANNE *off* : The police des . . .
FERDINAND *off* : People look at them suspiciously.
MARIANNE *off* : There was there . . .
> *Extreme close-up of a young man who speaks about himself directly into the camera.*
YOUNG MAN : Lazlo Kovacs, student, born 25th January, 1936 at St. Domingo, exiled by the American invasion, living in France as a political refugee; France, the country of Liberty, Equality, Fraternity . . .
> *Extreme close-up of a young woman who speaks directly into the camera.*
YOUNG WOMAN : Viviane Blassel, born 21st March, 1943 at Marseilles. Er . . . I'm twenty-two years old and I work at the perfume counter in a large store at Auxerre.
> *Extreme close-up of an old man.*
OLD MAN : Eté Andre, born 25th May, 1903 at Eure-et-Loire. Sixty-two years old. At this moment employed as a film-extra.
> MARIANNE *and* FERDINAND *are sitting on a step in front of a blue door; they look as if they are talking to each other, but they are not.*
FERDINAND *off* : Let's tell them some stories. They will feel sorry for us when we move them with words.
MARIANNE *off* : But what shall we say?
FERDINAND *off* : It doesn't matter. The Siege of Constantinople . . . or the story of Nicolas de Staël committing suicide. I don't know . . . or the one about William Wilson, who met his double in the street one day, and then searched everywhere for him, to kill him. When he'd eventually done it, he found out he had killed himself, and it was his double who was still alive.

MARIANNE *off* : Okay, they might give us some money after all . . .

Medium shot of MARIANNE, *talking to* LAZLO, *the* OLD MAN *and another man at a café table, outside. She is gesticulating wildly, embellishing her weird and wonderful tales with dramatic gestures, to enhance her hold over her audience* . . .

FERDINAND *off* : Marianne, who has the eyes of both Aucassin and Nicolette, told them the story of the young and handsome Vivien, nephew of William of Orange, killed on the plains of Aliscan by the bullets of three thousand Sarrazines. His blood flowed from a thousand wounds and yet he battled on alone, having vowed not to retrace a single step. Oh ! . . . so young and handsome, why such a vow so noble, yet so mad?

Medium shot of FERDINAND *talking to the young girl and her boyfriend, who continue to drink, obviously bored.*

MARIANNE *off* : At first, Ferdinand told them the story of Guynemer, but they weren't listening. So then he told them about the summer, and the desire that lovers have to breathe the cool evening air.

Long-shot of the sea in bright sunlight.

Close-up of a painting by Renoir of a nude girl.

Same long-shot of the sea, the sun glistening on the waves.

MARIANNE *off* : He spoke to them of man, of the seasons, of unexpected encounters, but he warned them never to ask what came first : words or things, or what would happen to us afterwards . . .

FERDINAND holds out his hand expectantly to his audience but receives nothing.

Long-shot as they return to their car parked in front of the café. The car is hemmed in by a car in front and another behind. FERDINAND *starts the car and lurches forward, hits the car in front, slams his into reverse and hits the car behind which is unceremoniously shoved back a few feet. Now he has room to get out. The people in the café have leapt to their feet but have little time to protest. His car tears out into the street and they drive away . . . as* MARIANNE'S *voice is heard* . . .

MARIANNE *off* : I feel alive, that's all that counts!

Quick shock-cut of two cars driving in different direc-
tions, as if straight into each other . . .

Close-up of the comic-strip cartoon characters in the
large book they have had with them throughout the film:
a hard cover edition of the well known comic that all
French children read, ' La Bande des Pieds Nickelés.' As
the camera pans across a page of the book, we see the
three heroes, ' Croquignol ', ' Filochard ' and ' Ribould-
ingue.' Piano music.

Long-shot as the car comes to a halt on a wild deserted
road between an avenue of plane trees, and far from any
signs of habitation. They get out of the car on each side
and take a closer look at something happening off screen
to the left.

MARIANNE : I've an idea.

FERDINAND gets back in the car and she moves off left,
followed by FERDINAND driving the car. As the camera
pans after them we see the remains of a wrecked car.
It has crashed vertically against a pylon, and the bodies
of a man and a woman are hanging out of the door
and window, smothered in blood.* FERDINAND drives their
car round close to the wreck. MARIANNE jumps round
excitedly, delighted by the good idea she has just had.

MARIANNE : We can make it look like an accident and then
the police will think we have been killed. Eh, Pierrot?

He gets out of the car and slams the door. He does not
share her indifference or enthusiasm. Disgruntled as
usual, he refuses to be called Pierrot.

FERDINAND : My name is *Ferdinand!* My name is *Ferdinand!*

Medium long-shot of FERDINAND getting back into the
car to drive it even closer to the wreckage, at her com-
mand. She runs back onto the road, looking round ex-
citedly to see if there are any police cars or unwanted
witnesses in sight. They argue as he gets out of the car
and takes their belongings from it, handing them to
MARIANNE.

MARIANNE : Come on . . . listen. There's nothing to it!

* Editor's note : the still on page 12 is a production still.

50

FERDINAND : What?

MARIANNE : Set the 404 on fire, so they'll believe we've been burnt too.

FERDINAND : Ugh . . . always fire, blood, war . . .

MARIANNE : But listen, it's my idea isn't it? Drive it nearer still! You know, make it look authentic. We're not in the cinema you know! But nearer, nearer . . . and hurry up!

He finally gets it near enough for her satisfaction. He takes the last things from the back seat and goes to collect a few things from the boot.

FERDINAND : Damn, I've no matches, let's go . . .

MARIANNE : That's no problem. Give me the gun.

FERDINAND : Christ! It's the same type that killed Kennedy.

MARIANNE : Yeah, didn't you know it was me? Look, get out of the way, I'm going to shoot.

FERDINAND *is trying to drag the case out of the boot of the car when she orders him to get out of the way.*

FERDINAND : But wait a minute!

He leaps back as she takes aim.

Medium close-up of MARIANNE *with the gunsights to her eye; she presses the trigger. The car explodes into flames, as he staggers up to her side, out of breath.*

MARIANNE : It burns jolly well, doesn't it?

FERDINAND : Yes, but you know what was in that case?

MARIANNE : No, what?

FERDINAND : Dollars . . . the ones you were looking for in the apartment.

MARIANNE : Stupid bastard . . . I'm sure you knew and didn't tell me on purpose!

FERDINAND : Right.

MARIANNE : But you realise what we could have done with all that money? . . . Gone to Chicago, Las Vegas, Monte Carlo . . . stupid bastard!

FERDINAND : Yes . . . me . . . Florence, Venice, Athens. Come on . . . let's get going. Travelling is the essence of youth.

She is heartbroken, and stays looking at the car, thinking of all the money burning. He turns and walks away from her, towards the fields. She follows reluctantly.

Long-shot of the two cars, blazing magnificently at the

foot of what is now seen to be a sort of derelict road-
bridge, perhaps built in the war, but now serving no
useful purpose whatsoever. A bridge joining nowhere to
nowhere. The camera pans very slowly round to follow
them as they walk on into the far distance, the black
smoke from the burning gasoline slowly obscuring them.

FERDINAND *off* : Chapter Eight.

MARIANNE *off* : A season in hell.

FERDINAND *off* : Chapter Eight.

MARIANNE *off* : We crossed France . . .

FERDINAND *off* : . . . like spirits . . .

MARIANNE *off* : . . . through a mirror . . .

Long-shot of them walking down the middle of a river,
hand in hand; FERDINAND *still clutching the book under*
his arm. Sinister music. They seem happy on their river
adventure. The water gets deeper and deeper so they
move towards the bank and climb out.

Long-shot of them sitting beneath trees, protected from
the world by the evergreen woods and glades of the
Loire valley landscape. They get up and dance along,
lyrically, happy and free. The music continues in sinister
counterpoint to their mood. (Still on page 30)

Long-shot: they cross a deserted road and continue
their tramp through the countryside. MARIANNE *is now*
wearing a U.S. Army jacket over a red woollen pullover.

FERDINAND *off* : Like spirits . . .

MARIANNE *off* : . . . through a mirror . . .

FERDINAND *off* : I saw the café where, one terrible night . . .
Van Gogh decided to cut off his ear.

MARIANNE *off* : Compère, you're lying. What did you see?

FERDINAND *off* : I saw . . .

Close-up: painting by Van Gogh of ' Café by night'.
Medium shot: they are sitting in front of a ' TOTAL '
petrol pump at a garage.He is reading the book, wearing
a gangster style hat and double breasted suit. She takes
the cigarette from his lips and smokes it . . .

MARIANNE : Look Pierrot, a Ford Galaxie !

FERDINAND : My name is Ferdinand. Yes . . . a '62.

MARIANNE : Go on, show me you're a man.

FERDINAND : Wait! When I've finished. *He reads*: 'Having covered quite a distance they arrived in sight of the Bayorda desert which they had to cross in order to get to Khartoum. ' Damn there's no shade ' cursed the Pieds-Nickelés, venturing into the tract of sand beneath the scorching sun. ' We'd have been much more comfortable and better off in the shade.' '

MARIANNE : Make up your mind or I'll hitch-hike on my own.

FERDINAND : Okay . . . let's go.

Long-shot of FERDINAND *helping her up from the ground and again they dance and fool around as they make their way towards a huge open American car just being driven into the garage.*

Medium long-shot: he beckons to her as they creep round the car. Its occupants, a man and a woman, get out and go into the garage.

TOURIST : Give it a service! . . . where are the toilets? . . . *To his wife* ' Okay, come on Mimi . . .'

MARIANNE *hides behind the car. She then creeps round it and* FERDINAND *opens the door for her. She slips into the car as the mechanic comes up.*

FERDINAND *talks to him as the car goes up on the pneumatic hoist. He moves under the car and turns it round so it is facing outwards.*

FERDINAND : Wouldn't you fancy a car like that, eh, son?

MECHANIC : You bet I would.

FERDINAND : Well, you'll never have one.

He calls up to MARIANNE *in the car to throw him down its owner's jacket from which he takes the money to bribe the mechanic to let the car down. Dramatic music.*

FERDINAND : Marianne! The coat! Hey kid . . . wouldn't you like to earn yourself ten thousand francs?

He gives the money to the boy, who lets out the pressure from the machine and the car comes slowly and painfully down. FERDINAND *gets into the car as it reaches ground level, starts the engine and drives it away from the garage like a lunatic, surging out into the road with screeching tyres.* MARIANNE *waves happily to the world as they speed away in their stolen American car.*

Cut to shot of the clear sky with the sun blazing down.

FERDINAND *off*: The countryside gradually becomes more mountainous . . .

MARIANNE *off*: Century after century plunged into the distance like tempests . . .

Long-shot: the car drives off the main road down a side road and then into a grass clearing. MARIANNE *jumps out while the car is still moving, and flings their old clothes into the nearby bushes.*

FERDINAND: Go on, chuck the clothes away while I turn the car round . . . Yippee! . . . The Pied-Nickelés!

MARIANNE: Hurry up . . . hurry up!

FERDINAND *turns the car round without stopping, and she runs after him . . . just managing to leap into the car as it careers back towards the main road.* MARIANNE *is now wearing a mauve-striped dress obviously stolen from the car.*

Long-shot: a police car with horn blaring and yellow light flashing, drives down a narrow road between white cottages.

Neon signs flashing 'VIE' (part of a sign saying 'RIVIERA.')

Medium close-up through the front windscreen of the car, as FERDINAND *drives along the country roads of Southern France.* MARIANNE *is reading a newspaper.*

FERDINAND: So?

MARIANNE: Nothing special! They interrogated her. She said she had seen us together, naked, in my bed. You see . . . you thought I was a liar!

FERDINAND: Isn't there anything else?

MARIANNE: Come on, admit it, you're still pretty interested in your wife, really!

Short flashbacks from the Party scene, early in the film at Madame Expresso's.

Shot of wife introducing FERDINAND *to* MARIANNE.

Yellow image of group of guests talking and drinking.

Shot of FERDINAND *on the bed as his wife throws the towel in his face.*

WOMAN IN RED: Nothing particular had happened. I don't understand it at all. He's just gone mad, that's all.

Image as before, the two of them in the car, seen through the front windscreen.

FERDINAND: Ah well, when you ditch a woman, she says you've gone out of your mind.

MARIANNE: Oh . . . with men . . . it's all bullshit!

FERDINAND: True . . . by the way, I've no idea why, I've begun to sense . . . the feeling of . . . death everywhere . . .

She turns on the car radio so loud that they have to shout to each other over the noise.

MARIANNE: Tell me you're sorry. Go on, say it, say it.

FERDINAND: Oh, shut up, for heavens sake! You're getting on my nerves . . . No . . . The smell of death in the countryside, in the trees, in the faces of women, in cars . . .

MARIANNE: You know we're going to be really fucked up without money — we can't even reach Italy!

FERDINAND: Well, we'll just have to come to a stop . . . wherever we are. There's no alternative but to stop wherever we are.

Same scene in car, from behind.

MARIANNE: And what will we do all day? No . . . it's vital that we find my brother first of all; he'll give us plenty of loot . . . and then we'll find a chic little hotel . . . and enjoy ourselves!

FERDINAND *turning round and speaking direct into the camera*: You see! . . . that's all they think about, enjoying themselves!

MARIANNE *also looking round, puzzled*: Who are you speaking to?

FERDINAND: To the audience.

MARIANNE: You see, I told you so . . . you are sorry already. You're mad to have done it.

FERDINAND: No, I'm in love.

MARIANNE: That's the same thing.

She leans over and kisses him gently on the neck.

MARIANNE: Personally, I decided never to fall in love again. I find it disgusting.

FERDINAND: No, don't say that! Don't say that . . . not that.

Same shot seen from the front again. She is leaning her

head on his shoulder as he drives with one arm around her.

FERDINAND : Ten minutes ago, I could see death everywhere, now it's the opposite. Look . . . the sea, the waves, the sky . . . Ah . . . life may be sad but it's always beautiful. Suddenly I feel free. We can do exactly what we want to do. Just watch . . .

He swings the wheel of the car from side to side, violently, arrogantly, rocking the car from side to side of the road.

FERDINAND : To the right . . . to the left . . . left, right . . .

MARIANNE : Little fool . . . little fool. He's following a straight line and he's got to stay with it right to the end.

FERDINAND : What! Then watch . . .

Very long-shot: the car swings from the road and drives across the grassy slope between the road and the sea. But the car does not stop. FERDINAND *drives it straight into the sea.*

FERDINAND *off* : Chapter Eight.

MARIANNE *off* : A season in hell.

The sky, bright sun, and loud romantic music.

FERDINAND *off* : Love has to be invented all over again.

MARIANNE *off* : True life lies elsewhere. Century after century plunge into the distance like tempests.

FERDINAND *off* : I held her close to me . . . and began to cry.

MARIANNE *off* : It was the first . . . it was the only dream.

Long-shot: they are hastily getting themselves and their belongings out of the car as it gradually drifts out to sea, sinking. (Still on page 29)

Neon sign flashing ' RIVIERA.'

FERDINAND *off* : So, are you coming?

MARIANNE *off* : Yes.

The beach. FERDINAND *is sitting on the rescued suitcases.* MARIANNE *comes up and he gets up and follows her. They walk in single file along the beach, swinging their cases jauntily, their voices off.*

MARIANNE *off* : Where are we going?

FERDINAND *off* : To the Island of Mystery, like the ' Children of Captain Grant.'

MARIANNE *off* : And what shall we do there?

FERDINAND *off* : Nothing. We'll simply exist . . .

MARIANNE *off* : Oh! la, la . . . that's going to be fun!

FERDINAND *off* : C'est la vie.

Close-up of the water's edge. Two pairs of bare feet walk through the water. The camera tracks along following their footprints in the wet sand, until no footprints remain, only some seaweed lapping to and fro in the water.

FERDINAND *off*: No, not at all. Fortunately I don't like spinach, because I would crave for it if I was deprived of it. I'd not be able to stand it. It's the same with you . . . except it's the opposite. There was a film like that with Michel Simon, where he allowed himself to be possessed by a girl.

MARIANNE *off* : So! Have you helped yourself by wanting to change your life?

FERDINAND *off* : I didn't say all that just to be infuriating.

Long-shot into the tops of the trees, and upwards into the sky.

MARIANNE *off* : In any case, you told me we'd see it right through to the end.

FERDINAND *off* : Yes. To the End of the Night.*

Medium shot: they are curled up on the beach asleep. It is night. MARIANNE *uncurls herself from him and, looking up at the night-sky, rests her head on* FERDINAND'S *body. As the camera pans up slightly, the flickering reflections of the moon on the sea come into the image.*

MARIANNE : You can see the moon very well, can't you?

FERDINAND : I don't see anything unusual.

MARIANNE : Oh, but I do. Me . . . I see a guy up there. Maybe its Leonov or that American . . . White.

FERDINAND : Yes, that's true, I see him as well. But it's not a Popoff or a nephew of Uncle Sam. I'll tell you who it is.

MARIANNE : Who is it?

FERDINAND : It's the man in the moon. And do you know what he's doing? He's crossing himself like mad.

MARIANNE : Why?

FERDINAND : Look.

MARIANNE : Why?

---

* ' Voyage au bout de la nuit ', a novel by Louis-Ferdinand Céline.

Long-shot of the moon.

FERDINAND : Because he's fed up. When he saw Leonov land on the moon, he was happy. At long last someone to talk to ! Since the beginning of time he's been the only inhabitant of the moon. But Leonov tried as hard as he could to force the entire works of Lenin into his head. So, as soon as White landed, on his trip, he went for refuge with the American. He'd not had time to say hello, before White stuffed a bottle of Coco-Cola down his throat, demanding that he said thank you beforehand. No wonder he's fed up. He's leaving the Americans and the Russians to fight their battles down below. He's getting out.

MARIANNE : Where's he going to go?

FERDINAND : He's coming here.

Close-up of MARIANNE *with her head in his lap. He strokes her hair slowly and gently, and bends down and kisses her shoulder. (Still on page 29)*

FERDINAND : Because he thinks you are very beautiful. He admires you . . . your arms . . . and your breasts . . . are very moving . . .

MARIANNE *quietly* : Stop it, stop it . . .

Long-shot of the sea. The camera pans up into the sky accompanied by grandiose music, building up to a huge climax.

MARIANNE *off* : Chapter Seven.

A bare stretch of sand. Suddenly two pairs of feet appear out of the sand, followed by arms, heads . . . they kiss each other, still half-covered with the sand under which they had buried themselves.

FERDINAND *off* : A poet, called revolver . . .

MARIANNE *off* : . . . Robert Browning . . .

FERDINAND *off* : . . . To escape from myself

MARIANNE *off* : . . . Never . . .

FERDINAND *off* : Darling . . .

MARIANNE *off* : As much as I will be myself . . .

FERDINAND *off* : And you will be yourself . . .

MARIANNE *off* : As long as we both remain together in this universe.

FERDINAND *off* : Me, who loves you.

MARIANNE *off* : And you who rejects me.

FERDINAND *off* : So much that one yearns to escape.

MARIANNE *off* : Which looks far too much like fate.

FERDINAND is sitting on a chair on the top of a cliff looking out to sea. He is still wearing white jeans and a striped madras cotton shirt. On his shoulder is a magnificently coloured parrot, which seems to be watching what FERDINAND is writing in his notebook.

Close-up of the pages in his notebook as he writes.

FERDINAND's *diary* : ' I have decided to keep a diary. Such is the essence of that being, face to face with nature, who is unable to believe. The urgency to describe it with language. We live by hunting and fishing. Tuesday : nothing. Friday. *In English* : my girl Friday. Experience of the flesh. The eyes; human countrysides. The mouth; onomatopoeias which disappear by becoming language. The language of poetry rises from the ruins. Friday; the writer decides to . . . *(word cut in half and incomprehensible)* . . . the freedom of others.'

FERDINAND looks up and sees MARIANNE climbing over the rocks towards him, carrying over her shoulder a long pointed stick, with a fish on the end which she has speared. (Still on page 30)

FERDINAND writing in his notebook, as previous image.

Close-up of words being written in the notebook.

Medium shot: FERDINAND puts the final touches to a home-made bow and arrow. He fires the crudely made arrow and there is a quick cut to MARIANNE walking along the beach with the fish, still in the air, on the end of the stick. She seems happy and gay, walking at the edge of the sea.

Close-up of the diary.

Long-shot: FERDINAND is driving a tractor with a flat trailer behind it, on which MARIANNE is dancing and leaping around. She is shouting and singing, but her voice is being drowned by the noise of the engine. She is dancing with a transistor radio in her hand and only just ducks down in time as they go under the low-hanging branch of a tree.

Close-up of the diary. The black writing is being corrected

by a red pen.
Long-shot: they are swimming in the sea and only their heads appear, very small at the bottom of the image.
Close-up of the diary. He is writing in red again.
Long-shot: FERDINAND *is sitting reading on a tree-trunk in the woods.* MARIANNE *comes up, her arms full of shopping.*
FERDINAND : Did you get the books?
MARIANNE : Not all of them, but I found some in the sale. The author has the same name as you.
FERDINAND : Oh, Ferdinand.
MARIANNE : You knew?
She throws him the books. He opens one and starts to read. Carried away by the words, and his own reading, he pompously mounts the fallen tree, shouting out the words to the whole world. (Still on page 31)
FERDINAND *reading*: ' I am the fire, I am the light, I am miraculous. I hear nothing any longer. I am rising . . . I pass by . . . through the air . . .' Ah! It's too much. ' I've seen happiness before me . . . supernatural emotion! '
FERDINAND *jumps off the tree to her side. She is carrying some bread and a few magazines. She soon gets bored with him reading, and breaks of some bread to eat. He circles round her, reading from the book in his left hand. He caresses her shoulders, her arms, and her hair.*
FERDINAND *reading*: ' And then . . . I know nothing any more . . . I go forward . . . inch by inch on my hands . . . and I dare . . . towards the right . . . I touch . . . I lightly stroke the hair of a fairy . . . of the wonderful, adored . . . Virginia! '
MARIANNE *is by now very bored with* FERDINAND'S *reading. She tilts up the cover of the book to read its title, and does so to insult him.*
MARIANNE : ' Guignol's Band '*! Right, are you coming?
She strides off leaving him to follow her, still reading from his book. He follows her down the trail towards their white stone cottage nestling under the cliff.
They reach the cottage and MARIANNE *flings the food on*

---

* A novel by Louis-Ferdinand Céline.

the wooden table in the patio and goes into the cottage through the open window.

FERDINAND *reading*: 'Sublime happiness! Ah! . . . I found myself in an ecstasy so intense that I dared no longer move. Happy to the point of tears, numbed by happiness I am quivering . . . quivering . . . How my heart is swelling, burning me. Unavoidably I burst into flames. I am in space . . . I cling to Virginia.'

FERDINAND *is now sitting in the patio. A tame fox and the parrot are sitting on the table.* MARIANNE *grabs the book from* FERDINAND'S *hands and starts to read from it herself, as a last resort to stop him reading.*

MARIANNE : Here, give it to me. *Reading*: 'You promised me China, Tibet, Mr. Sosthene . . . the island of Sonde, and magic exotic plants . . .' Where is all that now, eh?

FERDINAND *gives some food to the fox, and opens a bottle of beer for himself. As* MARIANNE *reads, she playfully bangs the fox on its head as if giving it a lesson.*

MARIANNE : Ah! ah! I am confronting him with his lies!

Close-up on the parrot which squawks loudly.

FERDINAND *off*: What day is it?

Close-up on the fox's face; it has just finished eating.

MARIANNE *off*: Friday.

FERDINAND *off*: You'll never leave me?

MARIANNE *off*: No, of course, not.

FERDINAND *off*: Of course, not?

Extreme close-up on MARIANNE, *looking very sad. After replying to* FERDINAND *she turns and looks straight into the camera and then back at him. She repeats her reply in a different tone, and looks into the camera again, then looks down, implying that she is lying and that she is a little ashamed of herself.*

MARIANNE : Yes, of course . . . Yes, of course . . .

Close-up of FERDINAND'S *diary.*

FERDINAND'S *diary*: 'Each picture, each book, presents its entire being to the freedom . . . audience . . . Thursday . . . poetry . . . he who loses wins'.

Long-shot: MARIANNE *is walking barefoot at the edge of the sea, shouting and crying to the winds, flinging stones into the sea, her legs wet with the water, her hair pulled up behind but wild-looking, and her eyes screwed up against the sun. The camera pans to follow her as she passes* FERDINAND *sitting on a ruined breakwater, writing in his notebook, his parrot perched on his knee.*

MARIANNE : What am I to do? . . . I don't know what to do! . . . What am I to do? . . . I don't know what to do! . . . What am I to do? . . . I don't know what to do! . . .

FERDINAND *shouts at her as she walks past, and then he reads out loud to the parrot from his diary.* MARIANNE *comes and sits at his side, rests her body against his, pokes her finger at the beak of the parrot and sighs out loud . . . she is desperately and agonisingly bored. He is completely absorbed in his writing . . . she rests her forehead limply on his shoulder as he continues to read.*

FERDINAND : Keep still, I'm writing! . . . ' In the end that is what it's all about . . . You are waiting for me . . . I'm not there . . . I arrive . . . I come into the room . . . I no longer really exist for you from that moment . . . whereas, before, I was alive . . . I was thinking . . . I was suffering perhaps . . . That is what it is all about, to show you are alive thinking of me . . . seeing me at the same time, alive for that very reason.' I'll underline that.

Close-up of the writing in the diary. Voices off over the words on the page.

FERDINAND *off* : Are you still thinking about your brother and the story about arms?

MARIANNE *off* : No.

Close-up : FERDINAND *turns to her and they talk quietly, with resignation. (Still on page 32)*

FERDINAND : Why do you look unhappy?

MARIANNE : Because you talk to me with words and I look at you with feelings.

FERDINAND : It's impossible to have a serious conversation with you. You never have ideas. Always feelings.

MARIANNE : But that's not true! There are ideas in feelings.

FERDINAND : Good. We will try to have a serious conversation. You are going to tell me what you love, what you desire . . . and I'll do the same. Okay then, you start.

62

MARIANNE : Flowers . . . animals . . . the blue of the sky . . . music . . . I don't really know . . . everything . . . and you?

FERDINAND : Ambition . . . hope . . . the movement of things . . . accidents . . . and what else? . . . I don't know . . . everything.

Long-shot of the same scene. Lethargically she leaves his side and walks away to the edge of the sea, once again flinging stones in the water, still unhappy and bored.

MARIANNE : You see I was right five years ago. We will never understand each other. What am I to do? . . . I don't know what to do . . . What can I do? . . . I don't know what to do . . . What am I to do? . . . I don't know what to do . . .

Close-up of FERDINAND'S *writing in the diary, with many more scribbles this time.*

FERDINAND'S *diary* : ' Saturday . . . eroticism . . . it is possible to . . . approbation of life . . . death . . . *He crosses this word out* . . . Sunday, she opened the . . . and afterwards . . . Monday . . . very . . . I read very much . . .

Montage of images from comics and covers of paper-back novels.

Sinister music.

Cover of a detective novel.

Photograph of a soldier.

Cover with a picture of a girl and the word ' DEATH '

MARIANNE *off* : How are you doing, old man?

FERDINAND : I'm all right!

FERDINAND *is sitting in the patio against a white wall. He talks straight into the camera imitating the voice and mannerisms of Michel Simon.*

FERDINAND: I've found an idea for a novel. No longer to write about people's lives . . . but only about life, life itself. What goes on between people, in space . . . like sound and colours. That would be something worth while. Joyce tried, but one must be able, ought to be able, to do better.

Medium long-shot of the same scene. MARIANNE *joins him at the table, throwing more books, this time at his head. They have an argument.*

MARIANNE : Here are your books.

FERDINAND : But they're not what I asked for! There's one

63

missing. I asked for five books.

MARIANNE : I bought a record too, look ! . . .

FERDINAND : I told you only one record for every fifty books. Music comes after literature !

> *He grabs the record and flings it to the ground. She looks at him as though this is the last straw, shouts at him — and stamps on the record to destroy it.*

MARIANNE : If that's what you want, my friend . . . my dear friend ! I'll pay you in kind . . . You'll get your money's worth !

FERDINAND *off* : What's all this now?

> *Close-up on* MARIANNE. *She is alternately insolent and sad. She is on the verge of tears.*

MARIANNE : I know how to write moronic rhymes as well !

FERDINAND *off* : What's the matter, Marianne?

MARIANNE : I'm fed up ! I'm fed up with the sea, with the sun, with the sand, tinned food, everything ! . . . I'm fed up with wearing the same dress every day ! . . . I want to get away from here ! . . . I want to live ! . . .

FERDINAND *off* : What do you want me to do?

MARIANNE : I don't know, I want just to go. Anyway, I've thrown away the money we had to keep us for the winter.

FERDINAND *off* : Where did you throw it?

MARIANNE : Into the sea, you idiot !

> *Long-shot of the same scene. She grabs his books and flings them all over the place. He lights a cigarette, trying to look cool. As they argue, he puts his hand on her shoulder.*

MARIANNE : There you are !

FERDINAND : But you're mad, Marianne. If you want to leave here so much, at least we have to have money.

> *At the mention of money, she turns round and slaps him across the face.*

MARIANNE : There are lots of tourists who come in on the boats . . . We can steal some from them . . . Come on . . . Oh, come on, Pierrot !

FERDINAND : My name is Ferdinand.

> *He turns round and stalks off, hurt, feeling it is over between them . . . He climbs up onto the roof. She*

64

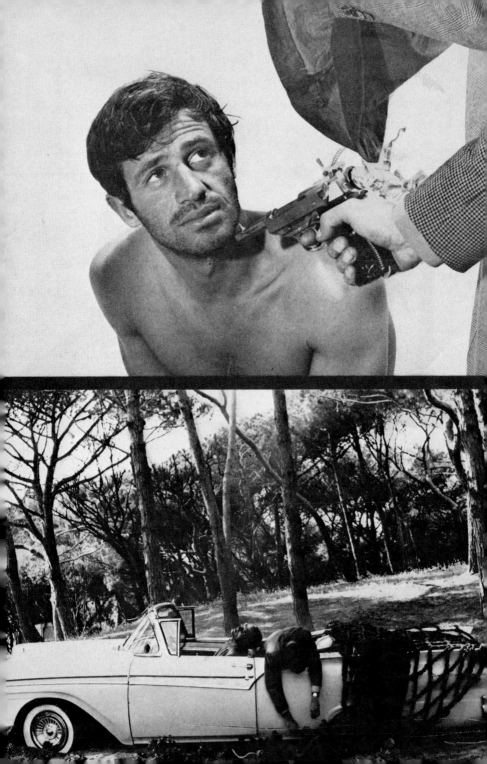

shouts up to him. He walks over the roof and the camera pans round following him as he runs down and jumps off, falling to the ground.

MARIANNE: Come on now, the Jules Verne novels are finished! Now we must start again like before with our detective stories . . . with cars, revolvers, night clubs. Come on! . . .

FERDINAND *picks himself up off the ground and runs after her to the beach. They walk along together, perhaps accomplices again.*

FERDINAND: Wait for me, Marianne! . . . Does your brother really exist then?

MARIANNE: You know, it's really funny! You never believe me.

Long-shot: the camera pans down the tall pine trees. They are walking together through the woods. FERDI-NAND *is still carrying his notebook and reading from it.*

MARIANNE: Listen, if we find Fred and he gives us some money, why don't we go to Miami Beach? . . . Deep down I think you are a coward.

FERDINAND: No. *Reading:* ' Courage consists in remaining inside oneself, next to nature, which holds no account of our disasters.'

MARIANNE: Are you going to hurry up? The tourist boat is about to leave.

FERDINAND *sits down on a fallen tree, determined to finish his writing. She saunters off along the fallen tree, balancing, but at the last minute turns and waits for him to stop writing.*

FERDINAND: Give me your lipstick. *Writing:* ' In the end, the only interesting thing is the part which human beings take. The tragedy . . . is that . . . once one knows . . . what one wants . . . where to go . . . what one is . . . everything still remains a mystery . . . '

MARIANNE: Like the smell of Eucalyptus.

FERDINAND: Eucalyptus, that's it.

MARIANNE: You don't say!

FERDINAND *writing:* ' And life . . . is this mystery . . . never resolved . . . '

MARIANNE : You get a move on, Paul!

FERDINAND : Shut up, Virginia!*

FERDINAND gets up and follows her.

Close-up of FERDINAND's diary.

FERDINAND's *diary*: 'Saturday . . . we are dead men on parole . . . the trees . . .'

Long-shot: camera pans across the pine trees as they run and walk along beneath them. The noise of the cicadas is deafening.

Close-up of the diary.

FERDINAND's *diary*: 'Saturday . . . 5 p.m. In order to get some money, we did some drawings for the tourists, some portraits of the champions of liberty.'

FERDINAND crosses out the word 'tourists' and writes instead 'modern slaves'. Sound of jet aeroplanes on soundtrack. Medium shot of MARIANNE and FERDINAND on their knees painting on one of the wooden jettys. They have drawn a huge portrait of Mao Tse-tung and inscribed it 'VIVE MAO'.

AMERICAN VOICE *off* : Hey, what are you doing there? Hey, you . . . hey, you.

MARIANNE *off* : Ah zut! Amerlocs!

Medium shot of American tourists, drinking whisky and reading detective novels and comics: a naval officer, a sailor and his girl.

FERDINAND : It doesn't matter; politics will have to be changed. Good, there's nothing else except . . .

MARIANNE : What?

FERDINAND : We can act a little theatrical sketch. Maybe they'll give us some dollars.

MARIANNE : Yes, but what?

FERDINAND : I don't know. Something that will amuse them.

MARIANNE : I know . . . the war in Vietnam.

Close-up of fire over water, a hand over the flames with a stick between the fingers — an approximation of a jet fighter.

---

* 'Paul et Virginie' by René Chateaubriand.

70

Hand against the sky with lighted matches — dive bombing. War sounds on the soundtrack.
Close-up: the American sailor enjoying it immensely, clapping and encouraging the performers.
Flames.
Matches fall into the water and are extinguished.
Medium shot of FERDINAND *dressed in the officer's uniform. He talks and gesticulates straight into the camera. In a terrible American accent he parodies his audience, biting out a cork from a whisky bottle and swigging the whisky. He points a gun at the camera on the sound of bombs dropping.*

FERDINAND : Sure . . . Yeah, yeah . . . New York . . . Oh yeah . . . Hollywood . . . Communist . . .

MARIANNE *is dressed in mock-Vietnamese costume and hat. Her face is painted yellow. She sings and talks in pseudo-Vietnamese getting more and more animated as the sound of bombs dropping gets louder.* FERDINAND'S *voice continues off with his Americanisms.*
Close-up of yellow paper and writing as in the diary.
'Uncle Sam's nephew versus Uncle Ho's niece.'
Short burst of machine-gun fire.

FERDINAND *is at a table slowly pouring himself a glass of whisky. Suddenly he turns round with his pistol and fires it time and time again at the Vietnamese* MARIANNE, *who comes wailing at him from the bushes, flailing her arms in the air.*
Close-up of the sailor laughing his appreciation.

SAILOR : Yeah man ! . . . I like that, that's good . . . damn good ! Yeah man ! I like that . . . yeah, yeah . . .

FERDINAND *in the uniform and the Vietnamese* MARIANNE *continue to fight and scream at each other.*
Close-up of tiger from a petrol advertisement.
Close-up of the red letters ' SS ' from ' ESSO ' sign.
Sounds of guns and war continue on the soundtrack.
They collect money from the audience. FERDINAND *is very disgruntled by the small amount given, but* MARIANNE *makes up for it by grabbing all the money from the officer's hand.*

FERDINAND : A little cash for the artistes!

AMERICAN : You know that did my heart good, fellow!

FERDINAND : Shit! Only one dollar.

MARIANNE : Don't worry, Pierrot.

FERDINAND : Down with Johnson!

AMERICAN : Eh! What are you doing there . . .

As MARIANNE *grabs the money they run away leaving the Americans shouting after them.*

MARIANNE : Long live Kennedy!

AMERICANS : Communists! . . .

Close-up of flames over the water, as the outraged voices of the Americans continue off-screen.

Close-up of their painting and the words ' VIVE MAO '.

Long-shot: they are still running away from the Americans. They stop breathless and start arguing. In the end MARIANNE *is about to go off on her own.*

FERDINAND : There we are, I routed them. Come on, let's go back.

MARIANNE : No, listen, I want to go dancing.

FERDINAND : No . . . come on with me, you can go tomorrow.

FERDINAND *off* : Next Chapter . . . Despair.

MARIANNE : No, I'm staying here.

FERDINAND : Okay then, I'm going back alone.

FERDINAND *off* : Hope . . .

MARIANNE : Yes, that's it then.

FERDINAND *off* : The search for lost times . . .

Close-up of MARIANNE *talking into the camera.*

MARIANNE : I was told they have dancing on the other side . . . I'm going dancing. Too bad if we get killed. They will find us anyway . . . and then? I wanted to buy myself a gramophone on Tuesday. I couldn't do so because he bought himself some books. Anyway, I don't give a damn, but he doesn't seem to understand that at all. I don't give a damn about books, about records, I don't give a damn about *anything,* even money . . . What I want is to be alive.

Long-shot: they are walking together through the tall pine trees.

MARIANNE *off* : But he'll never understand what it means to be alive.

The introductory music for a song fades up as they are wandering along in the woods together. He is slouching along with his hands in his pockets. She starts to sing and dances round him excitedly until he catches her mood and starts to act out the words of the song, going down on his knees and kissing her on the hip as she points gloomily at the lines on her hand. (Still on page 32)

MARIANNE *singing :* I've only a little line of luck,
I've only a little line of luck.
So little luck in my hand
That it makes me afraid of tomorrow.
My line of luck, my line of luck . . .
Tell me, my love what do you think?

FERDINAND *singing :* What do I think? What does it matter?
It's silly, but I love the line of your hip,
The line of your hip . . .

MARIANNE *singing :* My line of luck . . .

FERDINAND *singing :* I want to caress it with my hands,
The line of your hip!

MARIANNE *singing :* My line of luck!

FERDINAND *singing :* It's a flower . . . in my garden!

MARIANNE *singing :* But look at my tiny line of luck . . .
But look at my tiny line of luck . . .
Look at this tiny destiny,
So small, in the palm of my hand.
My line of luck, my line of luck . . .
Tell me, my love, what do you think?

FERDINAND *singing :* What do I think? What does it matter?
Be quiet and give me your hand.
The line of your hip . . .

MARIANNE *singing :* My line of luck . . .

FERDINAND *singing :* It's a bird in the morning,
The line of your hip . . .

MARIANNE *singing :* My line of luck,
The frivolous bird . . . of our destiny.
Even such a little line of luck,
Even such a little line of luck,
Such a little line of luck is better than
none.

It's scarcely even a mark on my hand.
My line of luck, my line of luck . . .
Tell me, my love, what do you think?
FERDINAND *singing* : What do I think? What does it matter?
I'm mad with joy,
Every morning!
The line of your hip . . .
MARIANNE *singing* : My line of luck . . .
FERDINAND *singing* : A bird sings in my hands.
The line of your . . .
MARIANNE *singing* : . . . hip . . .
FERDINAND *singing* : The line of my . . .
MARIANNE *singing* : . . . luck.

Medium shot of FERDINAND, *in a khaki uniform, sitting in a field of grass, which is higher than his head. Very slowly but emotionally, he talks straight into camera.*

FERDINAND : Perhaps I am dreaming even though I am awake . . . Her face makes me think of music. We have entered the age of the Double-Man. One no longer needs a mirror to speak to oneself. When Marianne says ' it is a fine day ' what is she really thinking? I have only this image of her, saying ' it is a fine day '. Nothing else. What is gained by trying to explain this? We are made of dreams . . . and dreams are made of us . . . It is a fine day, my love, in dreams, in words, and in death. It is a fine day, my love . . . It is a fine day . . . in life.

Long-shot of a broad river. FERDINAND *and* MARIANNE *are sitting on the bows of a small fishing boat which is being steered up the river by a fisherman.*
Medium close-up: sitting on the boat, MARIANNE *still holding her little woolly toy dog, has a pink rose between her breasts. She is making up her face.*

FERDINAND : You know what I'm thinking?
MARIANNE : Couldn't care less.
FERDINAND : Oh, Marianne, let's not start all over again!
MARRIANNE : I told you to leave me alone. Anyway, I'm not starting all over again, I am continuing.

Someone shouts at them from the quay. MARIANNE *looks up from her mirror and is suddenly angry.*

74

MARIANNE : Oh shit!

FERDINAND : What is it?

MARIANNE : Shit! shit! shit!

FERDINAND : What the hell is happening?

*Long-shot: the quay, seen from the travelling boat.
Running along the quay is the MIDGET, seen earlier in
the film when MARIANNE and FERDINAND were leaving
the apartment in Paris. He is wearing a captain's uniform,
and running with him is a girl in blue jeans and a blue
and white striped pullover. The MIDGET is jumping up
and down in excitement. As he shouts towards the boat,
he takes the girl's hand, pulling her towards the point
where the boat is going to reach the quay.*

Close-up of MARIANNE and FERDINAND on the boat.

MARIANNE : You know what you ought to write in your
novel?

FERDINAND : No, what?

MARIANNE : About somebody taking a walk in Paris . . .
suddenly he sees death . . . so, he promptly sets out for the
Midi to avoid confronting it again . . . because he thinks that
his time has not yet come.

FERDINAND : And then?

MARIANNE : Then he drives through the night as fast as he
can and in the morning he arrives at the sea. He gets a lift
in a lorry, but gets killed . . . just at the moment when he
thought death had lost track of him.

*As she is talking to him of death, their boat passes under
a bridge and their faces go dark in its shade.*

*Long-shot of the boat as it comes into land at the little
inland port. She stands up on the bow of the boat as it
drifts towards the camera. She shields her eyes from the
blazing sun. She jumps off the boat before it stops, turning to FERDINAND to make him hurry up. He hesitates,
but she drags him off as he flings some coins into the
boat for the fisherman.*

MARIANNE : Come on, hurry up!

FERDINAND : We've got plenty of time!

MARIANNE : No, no, I am afraid. You stay there.

MARIANNE forbids him to follow her as she goes to speak

to the MIDGET, *who by now is leaning against a sports-car and shouting into a walkie-talkie.*

MIDGET : You see, people always meet again in this life.

MARIANNE : What do you want?

She goes back to FERDINAND *who is obviously ready to beat up the* MIDGET. MARIANNE *leads him to one side, takes his hand, and ruffles his hair before she leaves him. She dances a couple of steps for his benefit, as she walks away along the quay.*

MARIANNE : I'll be back in five minutes.

FERDINAND : If you want I'll beat the hell out of him.

MARIANNE : No, no, I'm going to tell him some lies to get rid of him. I have to find out where Fred is, Pierrot.

FERDINAND : My name is Ferdinand. Okay, okay . . .

MARIANNE : Okay Mambo . . .

FERDINAND *goes off alone towards a restaurant near the beach. The girl in the striped jumper follows him, as the* MIDGET *has gone off with* MARIANNE.

MARIANNE'S *voice from far off, out of frame* : Pierrot, Pierrot! . . .

He hardly turns round as he walks away . . .

Close-up of the diary.

FERDINAND'S *diary* : ' Eroticism in this sense, betrays . . . nostalgia of a continuity . . . contradicts our separation . . . clears divisions . . . this desire of . . . *the next word is crossed out* . . . part also tied with . . . and the murder . . .'

Long-shot: FERDINAND *enters the restaurant through an open window. It is empty except for red painted wooden tables and chairs and a Mercedes car mysteriously parked in front of the bar. Music blares from the juke-box . . .*' Everything is going badly, Madame la Marquise, everything goes badly '.

FERDINAND *goes to the bar as the girl in the striped jumper comes in through the door. She goes straight to the juke-box and starts dancing to the music.*

FERDINAND : Two beers.

BAR GIRL : Two?

FERDINAND : Yes. When I finish one, I'll still have another, you see.

FERDINAND *picks up a newspaper from one of the tables and sits down at another table near the car. A man in a red pullover comes up to the table, slaps* FERDINAND *on the back and sits down next to him.*

MAN : You remember me? Last year at Fontainebleu you stayed at my place . . . I lent you 100,000 francs . . . you seduced my wife.

With the last remark FERDINAND *remembers the situation.*

FERDINAND : Yes, that's right!

MAN : So, you're in the Midi, then?

FERDINAND : Yes, I'm here on the coast.

MAN : You're all right?

FERDINAND : I'm fine.

MAN : Cheerio, then . . .

The man gets up and leaves FERDINAND *who drinks his beer and reads his newspaper.*

BAR GIRL : Are you Mr. Griffon?

FERDINAND : Yes.

BAR GIRL : You're wanted on the telephone.

FERDINAND *goes to the bar, picks up the telephone and listens. After a pause he replies.*

FERDINAND : My name is Ferdinand. It's me!

Medium shot: MARIANNE *on the telephone in a room with white stone walls and a reproduction of a Picasso painting behind her.*

MARIANNE : I'm all screwed up. They are completely mad, you know . . . I promise you, it's no joke.

MARIANNE'S *conversation is interrupted by sounds of the walkie-talkie. She puts the telephone down hastily as the* MIDGET *comes through the door behind her, a large Coca-Cola bottle in his hands. She grabs a newspaper and holds it in front of her face as he picks up the walkie-talkie and shouts incoherently into it. He takes a piece of paper from a typewriter on the table between them and reads from it into the walkie-talkie. He moves past* MARIANNE *who snatches the paper from his hand, but he manages to grab it back. The camera pans with him as* MARIANNE *puts down the newspaper and watches him, obviously determined not to let him out of her sight.*

Without him noticing, she takes out a pair of scissors and hides them behind the newspaper.

The MIDGET *puts the walkie-talkie down on a huge wooden crate which is standing below a 'Playboy' pin-up on the wall. He takes a number of files from the top of the crate as he shouts into the other room to* MARI-ANNE. *He begins removing a number of rifles, revolvers, and automatic weapons from the crate.*

MIDGET : If you don't tell me where you put the money, you're going to see . . . we'll torture you with electricity like during the war. And then, like in Vietnam, we'll strip you and put you in a bath full of napalm and set the whole thing alight.

Long-shot of FERDINAND *running out from the café towards the camera.*

MARIANNE *off* : No, make it quick if you don't mind.

Long-shot of FERDINAND *running across the end of a long street.*

MARIANNE *off* : You can kiss me however you like . . . I'll be very kind to you again.

Close-up of MARIANNE *on the telephone.*

MARIANNE : Then come quickly.

Long-shot of the beach. The camera zooms back sharply in three movements from close-up of FERDINAND *running along the beach, panning over the rooftops and ending in a medium close-up of* MARIANNE *on a balcony looking down at the beach. In her hand is the scissors which she ominously hammers on the parapet. The* MIDGET *comes up behind her and surprises her as he cocks the pistol in his hand, loads it with five bullets, and points it at her head. Sinister music. She bangs the scissors on the parapet, behaving as if she is not really scared, and ignores (Still on page 65) the pistol levelled straight at her head. She nonchalantly trims the split ends of her hair with the scissors . . .*

Long-shot of FERDINAND *running towards the tall apartment building where* MARIANNE *is being held prisoner. He half stops and looks up, shouting up to her that he is on the way to help her.*

Interior of apartment. Very wide angle distorted close-up of MIDGET; *his arm holding the pistol moves round until it points straight into the camera.*

Exterior long-shot of the tall building.

Interior. Very wide angle distorted shot of MARIANNE, *the scissors in her hand chop-chopping inches from the lens, from right to left, opposite to the movement of the* MIDGET *and the pistol. (Still on page 65) Medium shot of the ground floor of the building.* FERDINAND *rushes in and takes the lift, just as two* MEN *in light grey suits enter the building. The* TALL MAN *with fair hair and pale blue eyes is the one who was with the* MIDGET *at the beginning of the film. He is talking into a walkie-talkie set.*

TALL MAN : We'll have to walk up . . . *into walkie-talkie:* Hello, Jimmy . . .

FERDINAND breathlessly arrives through the door of the apartment and starts to look round. He picks up MARI-ANNE'S *red dress which is laid over the typewriter. On the floor he sees the* MIDGET *lying face downwards, dead, the scissors embedded in his neck. There is blood everywhere.*

FERDINAND kneels down and starts to take out the scissors.

Close-up of the MIDGET'S *head as* FERDINAND *pulls out the blood-stained scissors.*

FERDINAND : Beautiful, magnificent death for such a small man.

FERDINAND stands up pulling out the scissors with a jerk. He cleans the blood off them with MARIANNE'S *dress. As he does so, the* TALL MAN *enters the room behind him and stealthily moves towards the* MIDGET. FERDINAND *turns sharply and to his amazement, sees the* MAN *lift up the* MIDGET *by his feet and lay him unceremoniously over the back of a chair.* FERDINAND *makes as if to leave, but the* MAN *bars his way at the door.*

FERDINAND turns and tries to leave by the window that leads onto the balcony but is met there by the OTHER MAN.

TALL MAN : What are you doing here, my friend?

FERDINAND : I heard a noise — I live downstairs.

The OTHER MAN *advances and* FERDINAND *backs into the room.*

Close-up of the TALL MAN *with pale blue eyes, who walks slowly and menacingly towards camera, raising his right hand as if for a karate blow.*

Close-up in profile of FERDINAND *bracing himself for the blow.*

TALL MAN : Knock him down!

Close-up of the head from the Picasso painting on the wall.

OTHER MAN : We'll use your special method.

The Picasso head turns upside down. Agonizing screams and blows on the soundtrack.

OTHER MAN : See, kid? Who is the strongest . . . ?

Close-up of head of girl from another Picasso painting.

OTHER MAN *off* : What have you done with the money from the 404? . . .

TALL MAN *off* : That's it, into the bath.

The TALL MAN *leads* FERDINAND *towards the bathroom while the* OTHER MAN *goes to the window and signals with his hand to someone down below. He picks up a silver revolver. The* TALL MAN *sticks his head into the room and they both go off into the bathroom.*

TALL MAN *off* : Remember, we have to go and see the yacht.

OTHER MAN *off* : Listen, there is no towel.

TALL MAN *off* : We can use that little whore's dress. Don't strangle him . . . simply over the face so that the air can't get through when we use the water.

Close-up of FERDINAND *in the bath, the pistol pointed inches away from his chin. (Still on page 68)* MARIANNE'S *red dress is put over his head.*

OTHER MAN : Look pal, I'll help you by telling you what I know. Afterwards, I'll ask one question and I want a straight reply, without stalling. I know who you are. Your name is Ferdinand Griffon. You were with Marianne when she stabbed our friend Donovan, and you . . . you both fled with fifty thousand dollars which belongs to me.

Water is poured over FERDINAND'S *head from the hand shower, and he starts to choke. The water makes it impossible for him to breathe through the material of the dress. However, he deliberately replies stupidly.*

FERDINAND : Ploum ploum, tra la la . . .

OTHER MAN : Personally, I have nothing against you. I am sure it was Marianne who enticed you into this story, and that's your business. As I was saying, you don't interest me especially — she does, yes, and I'll get her. You're going to tell me exactly where I can find her, and the money.

They take off the red dress and FERDINAND *gasps for air.*

OTHER MAN : It's your last chance, either you tell me now, or you will be killed.

FERDINAND : Ploum ploum, tra la la . . .

The dress is put back over FERDINAND'S *head and the torture continues. When it seems as if* FERDINAND *can no longer breath they remove the dress once again and* FERDINAND *gasps out a reply.*

FERDINAND : At the Marquise night club.

OTHER MAN : Good. Either it's the truth or it's a lie. Anyway, he looks as if he will not tell us anything else. We will go and see.

FERDINAND : At the Marquise night club.

Close-up of FERDINAND'S *diary.*

FERDINAND'S *diary* : ' Maybe she panicked . . . Thursday . . . I was normal . . . I am going to . . . to hate but I never understood . . . about Marianne's loyalty . . .'

FERDINAND *slouches ponderously along a railway track next to a river. We hear the sound of a train approaching. He sits down between the tracks, unbuttons the jacket of his light-weight suit, and hangs his head between his knees.*

FERDINAND *off* : Ah! what a dreadful five in the afternoon . . . Blood, I do not want to see blood . . . Ah! what a dreadful five in the afternoon . . . I do not want to see it . . . I do not want to see the blood . . . Ah! what a dreadful five in the afternoon.*

---

* 'Lament for Ignacio Sánchez Mejvras' by Frederico Garcia Lorca.

The sound of the approaching train gets louder. There is a very long, loud hoot of the train's whistle. The camera pans to the right so that FERDINAND *is on the left of the screen. At the very last minute he staggers up from the ground and just escapes being hit by the train. The huge engine blasts past the camera. Through the wheels of the trucks we see him walking away towards the high grass beyond the railway line.*

MARIANNE *off* : We meet Ferdinand again as he reaches the station at . . .

FERDINAND *off* : Toulon.

Long-shot of the Toulon docks. The camera pans over the rubbish floating in the water and comes to rest on FERDINAND *sitting on the quay reading a newspaper. Their voices off continue the dialogue.*

MARIANNE *off* : We see him wandering around the streets and the harbour. He stays in . . .

FERDINAND *off* : The little Palace Hotel.

MARIANNE *off* : He is looking for . . .

FERDINAND *off* : Marianne.

MARIANNE *off* : He doesn't find her. Days pass by. In the afternoons Ferdinand sometimes sleeps in the cinema. He continues to write his diary.

Medium shot of FERDINAND *against a red and white sign on a wall: ' S.O.S. ' He lights a cigarette and flashes a look at the camera.*

FERDINAND *off* : For words in the midst of the shadows are a strange power of enlightenment.

MARIANNE *off* : Of the things they signify, in effect.

Close-up of a drawing of Rimbaud with coloured vowels dotted over his face . . . presumably an allusion to the poem of that name.

FERDINAND *off* : Even if they are compromised in day to day life.

MARIANNE *off* : Language often retains only purity.

Close-up of the diary with red lettering. FERDINAND *breaks down the word MARIANNE into the words ARIANNE, MER, AME, AMER and ARME.*

Medium shot: FERDINAND *in a cinema asleep in his seat,*

*in front of a couple of sailors. At the sounds of war he
wakes up and looks at the screen.*

COMMENTATOR : In Vietnam, the base at Da-Nang, which is
one of the principal strategic positions of the American forces,
was attacked by the Vietcong. The daylight raid destroyed
seven huts.

*On the cinema screen we see newsreel footage of the war
in Vietnam: a boat going through paddy fields . . . a
gun firing into the jungle, marines going into battle.*

COMMENTATOR: In the jungle, for the first time, the American
soldiers were fighting side by side with forces from South
Vietnam and Australia, in an all-out effort to reduce the
Vietcong resistance.

*FERDINAND is bored. He takes out the paperback history
of art he was reading at the beginning of the film. But
again he looks up at the screen.*

*On the screen a village hut is being set alight by the
soldiers, who are seen kicking the people as they escape
from the flames.*

COMMENTATOR : In spite of this extension of the conflict, and
the failure of the Commonwealth Peace Mission, Harold
Wilson has declared himself ready to intervene in an effort
towards eventual negotiations.

*FERDINAND reading his book. The camera tracks into
extreme close-up as we hear some voices from the screen.
We see scenes from Godard's short film ' Le Grand
Escroc '.*

MAN'S VOICE : Your story ends there.

WOMAN'S VOICE : Yes, he turned his back on me, leaving me
unhappy . . .

*On the screen Jean Seberg is holding a 16mm. movie
camera as she talks. Cut to the image she is photo-
graphing, which seems to be a long-shot of two people
on a donkey . . .*

WOMAN'S VOICE : We are carefully looking for . . . that
moment when one abandons the fictional character in order
to discover the true one . . . if such a thing exists.

*Very tight close-up of FERDINAND'S eye looking over the
book.*

*On the screen, the close-up of the three lenses of Jean
Seberg's camera.*

Ferdinand *is sitting on the quay of the port with the
yachts and small boats behind him. He is eating a huge
piece of cheese which he covers with mustard. He is
wearing sun glasses, a dark pullover and a cap.*

Princess *off* : I am the Princess Aicha Abadie, and in spite
of the fact that I look like a doll, from Tanagra, it's not true
. . . I have authority, and I do not like people to resist me.
I want them to obey me.

*Medium long-shot of the Princess, who is wearing a long
white stole over a pink dress, and lipstick as red as the
roses in her button-hole and hair. She is talking to a
young sailor who is coiling a rope patiently at her side.*

Sailor : So . . . Princess, what are the orders today?

Princess : I am Lebanese by adoption . . . in 1960 I married
the Emir Abadie. I am the Queen of the Lebanon in exile,
because you cannot ignore the fact that it is actually a
socialist republic. And so I am incognito in Nice because my
husband and I have terrible enemies and there is a price
on our heads in the Lebanon. Often I am shot at by machine
guns which do not injure me, because without doubt, I am
protected by Allah. In order to marry the Emir Abadie, I
had to convert to the Islamic faith. I have been to Beirut
twice in my husband's supersonic aeroplane.

Ferdinand *continues to eat his lump of cheese.*

*The Princess and the sailor start to move down the gang-
way. The Princess speaks to* Ferdinand.

Princess : And the Marabout of Atla . . . all right, Alexis?
Take care to stop me from floating away as there is quite a
tide . . and you know I am very light. Help me, Ferdinand.

*She holds her hand out to him. He puts down his cheese
and leads her with his two hands towards the quay.*

Princess : Ferdinand, we weigh anchor in an hour.

Ferdinand : Very good, Princess.

Princess : Alexis, we will go into the town.

*The sailor puts her coat around her shoulders and leads
her away.*

Ferdinand *goes back to recover his cheese when he hears*

MARIANNE's *voice shouting to him.*

MARIANNE *off* : Pierrot, Pierrot!

He stops and looks past the camera into the distance. He walks back down the plank and comes close-up into the camera.

He does not seem particularly pleased at what he sees . . .

Long-shot: MARIANNE *is sitting on a capstan wearing trousers, a sailor hat and a grey pullover tied around her neck.*

She gets up and pirouettes around a flagpole, then they walk round each other somewhat embarrassed at seeing each other again.

MARIANNE : Pierrot, it's me . . .

FERDINAND : My name is Ferdinand . . . Salut!

MARIANNE : You don't seem terribly surprised to see me.

FERDINAND : What are you doing here?

MARIANNE : I am happy . . . at last I've found you.

She pulls his hat down over his eyes. The camera pans to the right as she sits down again on the capstan. He joins her and they sit back to back.

FERDINAND : Where are you living at the moment?

MARIANNE : With you, of course, you idiot! I'm staying with you! I have been looking for you everywhere!

FERDINAND : You only had to wait for me . . . after telephoning.

Close-up on MARIANNE.

MARIANNE : But that's what I wanted to do. I managed to get out before the others arrived . . . then I ran to the bar to warn you not to come, but I didn't see you there. So then I returned and I saw the others getting into a light blue Ford, and I thought they had killed you. So afterwards . . . afterwards I went all over the place, I didn't know really where I was . . . and I was scared to go back to the coast. One day I met Fred by accident in a bar in Toulon . . . yes, yes . . . in the Las Vegas in Toulon.

FERDINAND : How did you find me here?

MARIANNE : By accident as well.

Medium shot of the two of them.

MARIANNE : It's true you know.

FERDINAND : I believe you, liar!

MARIANNE : But why do you never believe that I love you. I do love you . . . in my own peculiar way.

FERDINAND : Yes, that's just it!

MARIANNE : The proof . . . Look, yesterday I went down to our little beach and I picked up your notebook.

FERDINAND : Thanks.

MARIANNE : Look at the last page, there is a little poem about you. It's by me.

Close-up on FERDINAND *as he reads.*

FERDINAND : Tender . . . and cruel . . .
real . . . and surreal . . .
terrifying . . . . and funny
nocturnal . . . and diurnal
usual . . . and unusual
handsome as anyone

MARIANNE : Pierrot le Fou!

FERDINAND : My name is Ferdinand. I have told you often enough. Christ almighty! You bore me to death!

MARIANNE : If you think it's going to do you any good to scream ' Christ almighty ', you're wrong.

FERDINAND : God, that makes me . . .

MARIANNE : Don't talk that way!

Long-shot of them both. She starts putting on lipstick as she gets more and more bored with the conversation.

FERDINAND : You can talk . . . We're wanted for murder. Murder — do you know what that really means?

MARIANNE : Yes, of course, I know what it means. So? . . . Does it make you afraid? Tell me what . . .

FERDINAND : I am looking at you . . . I am listening to you . . . but that's not what is important.

MARIANNE : Oh! Thanks very much.

FERDINAND : No . . . I want to say at this precise moment before it's already in the past . . . I don't know . . . the colour of the blue sky . . . the rapport between us . . .

MARIANNE : I don't understand.

FERDINAND : The only thing I want is for time to stop. You see, I put my hand on your knee which is marvellous in itself . . . that is life. Space . . . feelings . . . but instead of that I

will follow you, and continue our story of blood and thunder.
It's the same for me either way . . .

MARIANNE : You're coming? Fred is waiting for us.

FERDINAND : Okay, I said nothing at all. Allons-y, alonzo . . .

*MARIANNE jumps up and runs off and FERDINAND runs
after her.*

*Long-shot of the car park as they reach a dark blue, open
Alfa Romeo sports car. MARIANNE drives the car as
FERDINAND, with a big flourish, throws his hat high into
the air.*

FERDINAND : I don't really know what the police are up to.
We should have been in prison long ago.

MARIANNE : No, they are the stronger, they leave people to
destroy themselves.

Flashing neon sign ' CINEMA '.

*Long-shot: the car drives up outside a small compound.
MARIANNE sounds the horn and a guard jumps up and
opens the high wire gates. The camera pans with the
car as MARIANNE drives it towards a large motorboat
moored to the jetty.*

FERDINAND : Why do you do things like that?

MARIANNE : I've told you it wasn't me who killed him!

FERDINAND helps her to get out of the car.

*Same scene from another angle. They go over towards
the boat.*

FERDINAND : It's funny to be alive after seeing such a proces-
sion of corpses.

MARIANNE : Oh, yes, it's funny! Ha, ha, ha!

FERDINAND : It makes one think of the décor for Pepe-le-Moko.

MARIANNE : Who?

FERDINAND : Pepe-le-Moko.

MARIANNE : Who is that?

FERDINAND : Really . . . you don't know anything at all!

*They jump into the boat. FERDINAND stays at the helm,
acting as if he is revving up the engine. She goes up
front, still talking, and taps on the window. The motorboat speeds away.*

MARIANNE : And what about you? Do you know what you
are in the final analysis?

FERDINAND : Who, me? I am a man . . . of sensuality . . .

MARIANNE : Says you! *I* know what you are, but *you* don't.

FERDINAND : It's true. I am only a huge question mark poised over the Mediterranean horizon.

Close-up of FERDINAND's *diary. Blue paper.*

FERDINAND's *diary* : ' . . . Their truth, their truth . . . independent of us in . . . our logic and of . . . in knowing something . . .'

Close-up of MARIANNE *sitting at the back of the boat, her hair blowing in the wind, the sea behind her reflecting the sun as the boat ploughs through it . . .*

FERDINAND *off* : Are your parents still alive?

MARIANNE : Yes, they have never left each other. They almost separated once, though. Papa was going on a trip, I don't know where . . . anyway a very small trip. They didn't have enough money to buy two tickets. Mother accompanied him to the bus . . . they looked at each other. She was still down below, he at the window. At the moment the bus started to leave, Papa got down from the bus as quick as he could. He couldn't leave my mother. And as he was getting down from the door at the front, she got up by the door at the back. She couldn't bear to leave my father. In the end Papa decided not to go on the trip.

FERDINAND : What were you doing while you were working as a liftgirl?

MARIANNE : Oh nothing . . . I looked at people's faces.

FERDINAND : Where was it?

MARIANNE : Galeries Lafayette. Why all these questions?

FERDINAND : I am trying to know exactly who you are . . . I never knew, even five years ago.

MARIANNE : Oh! Me . . . I'm just very sentimental that's all. You really would be a fool to find that mysterious.

FERDINAND : And your brother, what does he do exactly? I never know whether you're telling stories or not.

MARIANNE : My brother . . . oh! you know!

FERDINAND : But what was he doing at Tel-Aviv?

MARIANNE : Well . . . listen, at this moment there is a war in the Yemen. You're really not up to date with anything. He gets money from the Royalist government.

FERDINAND : And the others? They work for the Arab League?

MARIANNE : One doesn't know. Almost certainly.

FERDINAND : He has a troupe of dancers, really?

MARIANNE : What's that to you?

FERDINAND : What's the point of having a cover for arms trafficking nowadays, when it's almost official?

MARIANNE : What's that to do with you?

FERDINAND : Tell me!

MARIANNE : Okay I'll tell you. In one hour there are three thousand, six hundred seconds. In one day, that makes around a hundred thousand. In an average life, that makes about two hundred and fifty milliards of seconds. Since we have known each other, we have been with each other for about a month. If we add that up, that means I have seen you only for one or two million seconds out of the two hundred and fifty milliards which make up your life. That's not very much. So it doesn't surprise me that we don't know who we are . . .

A long-playing record is playing on a portable gramophone, precariously balanced on a log near the edge of the sea. The loud music ceases abruptly when the water splashes onto the record.

Long-shot of a beach. A troupe of dancers are practising on the sand. In the foreground, MARIANNE hands a gun to a man in a red pullover and then joins the dancers. The young man in charge of the troupe comes up, puts his arms round her and kisses her. It is her ' brother ', FRED. She dances round enthusiastically. The camera tracks along the sand as MARIANNE and her brother walk along talking. The pop music continues and the dancers cavort around them madly like a Matisse painting come to life. They all shout out numbers in time with the music.

FRED : He wants to do it, really?

MARIANNE : Yes, he'll do anything I ask him. Oh! what a mic-mac . . . you know . . .

FRED : Six . . . seven . . . eight . . .

MARIANNE : It's fantastic! . . . One-two-three-four-five . . .

93

Close-up of FERDINAND's *diary. He makes corrections with a red pen.*

FERDINAND's *diary*: 'To see clearly . . . reason . . . with life . . .'

Long-shot of FERDINAND *sitting reading a newspaper at the foot of a tree in a forest clearing. A small white car drives up and* MARIANNE *and her brother,* FRED *get out.* FRED *shakes* FERDINAND's *hand, and they all walk away together.* MARIANNE *is playful and makes* FERDINAND *carry her red pullover.*

FERDINAND : What is it I have to do?

FRED : You will do what we tell you.

MARIANNE : Listen, open your eyes and your ears, and you'll see very clearly. You remember the scent of the Eucalyptus? *She strokes his hair and dances around him, as their voices, off, carry on the dialogue.*

FERDINAND *off* : It's always complicated with you.

MARIANNE *off* : No, everything is simple.

FERDINAND *off* : Too many things happen at the same time.

MARIANNE *off* : Not at all.

A long montage of short images follow, edited out of time sequence, which, accompanied by their voices off screen, gives an idea of the chaotic way in which FERDINAND *might remember the extraordinary events he has by accident been drawn into, in her real life game of cops and robbers . . .*

FERDINAND *off* : There is a little harbour, like in a novel by Conrad.

Long-shot from above of boats in the harbour.

MARIANNE *off* : A sailing ship, like in the novels of Stevenson. *The white boat, from right to left.*

FERDINAND *off* : An old brothel, like in the novels of Faulkner.

A car is being driven through the pine forest.

MARIANNE *off* : A waiter becomes a millionaire, like in the novels of Jack London.

Long-shot of the quay. A man wearing a captain's hat and uniform, with a white dog on a lead, walking up the gangplank from a boat and coming towards the camera.

FERDINAND *off* : It is always complicated with you.

MARIANNE *off* : No, everything is simple.

FERDINAND *off* : Too many things happen at once.

MARIANNE *off* : No.

FERDINAND *off* : There are two guys who beat me up, like in a Raymond Chandler novel.

MARIANNE *off* : And you . . . and me . . . and him . . . You see, it is simple.

The TALL MAN *with pale blue eyes and his friend are sitting in an open car. They pass a black case between them which is open, and we see it is full of dollars. The* OTHER MAN *checks it closely and hands it back to the* TALL MAN.

FERDINAND *off* : I see nothing at all.

MARIANNE *off* : They want to buy . . .

FERDINAND *off* : . . . the yacht

MARIANNE *off* : The old man is not . . .

FERDINAND *off* : . . . French.

The man with the dog gets into a dark blue Bentley helped by a driver wearing a gangster suit.

MARIANNE *off* : My brother cashed . . .

FERDINAND *off* : . . . the money

MARIANNE *off* : The others are not . . .

FERDINAND *off* : . . . aware of what's happening.

Long-shot of a red car. FRED *hands a gun to the driver inside.*

MARIANNE *off* : They are going to be . . .

FERDINAND *off* : . . . furious.

Long-shot of the dark blue Bentley. The TALL MAN *with the blue eyes arrives and hands over the case of dollars. The man in the Bentley hands out some documents which they all sign.*

MARIANNE *off* : They are going to follow Fred. We'll get rid of them.

FERDINAND *off* : And afterwards?

FERDINAND *at the wheel of the red car, lighting a cigarette, his elbow on the window-sill. He is anxious*

95

to leave. (Still on page 66)

MARIANNE *off* : You'll do what you're told.

Long-shot of the dark blue Bentley being driven very fast through the streets towards the harbour, closely followed by the open, grey American limousine containing the TALL MAN *and his friend.*

Neon signs flashing ' LAS VEGAS.' The sinister music suddenly stops and is followed by piano music. At the end of the neon signs the loud sinister music starts again.

Medium shot of MARIANNE *next to her blue car. She is kneeling down, looking through the telescopic sights of a rifle. (Still on page 67)*

Long-shot of a clearing in the pine forest. The Bentley and the American car drive into the clearing. A shot is fired and the Bentley drives off. Just as the grey American car starts to follow, a huge rope-net drops from the trees above it, covering the drivers and stopping the car. They struggle under the rope. The red car enters the clearing driven by FERDINAND.

Close-up of MARIANNE *with the gun up to her eye. Image seen through telescopic sights. The two men struggling under the rope net.* MARIANNE *moves the telescopic sight between the heads of the two men, looking, waiting for the moment to press the trigger.*

MARIANNE *off* : A woman can very easily kill people. It does not mean that because she has round breasts and soft thighs that she cannot massacre anyone she likes in order to remain free, or to defend herself. Look at Cuba . . . or Vietnam . . . or Israel . . .

MARIANNE manages to keep the TALL MAN'S *head in her sights long enough . . .*

Close-up of MARIANNE'S *face with the gun at her eye. She looks up, and then down into the sight again.*

The TALL MAN *is shot dead by* MARIANNE. *(Still on page 68)*

Close-up of MARIANNE *as she looks up again smiling at her success.*

Long-shot of the Bentley careering down the streets of

96

a town.

MARIANNE's blue car drives across right; FERDINAND's red car from the left. They circle round and round until they are close enough to lean out of their cars for a quick kiss, before they drive off madly again in opposite directions.

FERDINAND : I love you.

MARIANNE : Me too.

Long-shot: the Bentley and the red car drive past tall warehouses near the harbour. The red car stops and the Bentley crashes into it.

Medium shot: FERDINAND jumps out of the car with a gun in his hands. He is a bit dizzy from the impact as he lurches towards the Bentley. The driver sticks up his hands through the open sun roof. FERDINAND peers into the back of the car and sees that the man in the captain's uniform has been murdered. FRED is in the seat next to the driver, and shoots the driver in the back of the head. FRED hands the case with the dollars to FERDINAND, who gets back into his car and drives away.

FERDINAND *off* : Next Chapter . . . Despair . . . Next Chapter . . . Liberty . . . Bitterness . . .

Long-shot: FERDINAND's red car drives past two huge mounds of lime. The camera pans left to right; it is not horizontal so there is a strange distortion emphasising the drama . . .

Long-shot: the red car arrives outside a bowling alley. FERDINAND parks his car next to MARIANNE's and speaks to a little girl sitting on a table.

FERDINAND : Tell me, have you seen a young woman, looking like a Hollywood film star?

LITTLE GIRL : It's none of your business.

Interior of the bowling alley. MARIANNE, wearing blue corduroy trousers and a white T-shirt, is playing bowls. (Still on page 85) The camera pans left from MARIANNE to FERDINAND arriving, then pans right to MARIANNE who bowls. The camera tracks forward until the ball hits the skittles. It tracks back as the ball returns towards MARIANNE, and reaches her as she is taking off her soft shoes. She goes up to FERDINAND *who has sat down, with the case on his lap.*

MARIANNE : Is it all there?

FERDINAND : Yes.

MARIANNE : We'll meet again this evening as we arranged?

FERDINAND : Yes. Some people saw me.

MARIANNE : You idiot!

FERDINAND : I don't understand.

MARIANNE : Fred will appear innocent now.

FERDINAND : Why do you let me down?

MARIANNE : What's the matter?

FERDINAND : Nothing, I'm just looking at the woman who makes me suffer.

MARIANNE : But you know, Pierrot, fifty thousand dollars are enough to make anybody nervous.

FERDINAND : My name is Ferdinand. Why did you kiss me a few minutes ago?

MARIANNE : Because I wanted to.

FERDINAND : Kiss me again.

MARIANNE : Not in front of everybody.

> MARIANNE *tries to take the case from* FERDINAND'S *lap. In a flash, he clutches it like a maniac and puts it safe between his legs.* MARIANNE *shrugs her shoulders, putting on her shoes. She walks provocatively away from him.*

FERDINAND : Why do you wear such tight trousers?

> *She returns to him and tries to take the case. This time he grabs it very violently.*

MARIANNE : If that's the way you feel, my dear, why don't you go back to Paris?

FERDINAND : Kiss me.

MARIANNE : Right, I understand. You know, it's not going to be so good for you now you've given us away.

FERDINAND : Shut up, Cassandra.

MARIANNE : What?

FERDINAND : It's all right, it's only the title of a novel.

> *He picks up a detective novel lying on the table, and shows her the cover. She is furious and marches off leaving him alone hugging the case of money.*

98

MARIANNE : Stupid idiot!
He jumps up and follows her.
FERDINAND : Listen . . . Marianne . . .
Medium shot of MARIANNE *walking towards her car outside.*
He catches up with her and they talk, sitting on the cars.
MARIANNE : What?
FERDINAND : TWA Nice, 3.15 Tahiti. An aeroplane. Let's take it.
MARIANNE : Both of us, evidently, you mean both of us.
FERDINAND : Evidently, yes.
Close-up on MARIANNE *looking bored to death. She leans forward as his arm lingers behind her shoulder, uneasy about resting on it.*
MARIANNE : Evidently . . . it's funny in French . . . in the end, words often mean the opposite to what they are supposed to mean. We say ' evident ' about things which aren't evident at all.
FERDINAND : Yes, me for example, it was evident that I would not find the little old man from the yacht with a bullet between his eyes, and worse, it came out of the back of his skull. You know, don't you, that your brother killed him?
MARIANNE : That doesn't matter to me. Most of all I'd like to go away, I'd like to beat the hell out of here, but Fred would find us and get his revenge. I once saw him get his revenge on a girl.
FERDINAND : I'll protect you.
MARIANNE *goes ' boo boo ' at her little woollen toy dog.*
Close-up on FERDINAND *looking desolate.*
MARIANNE *off* : Good. I'll have to go alone, so that he won't suspect me.
FERDINAND : Okay, beautiful.
MARIANNE : Okay, handsome. Good . . . I'll go there since there's nothing more for us to say to each other. Meet me again in half an hour.
FERDINAND : No. I will count up to . . . 137.
MARIANNE : You are really mad.
Long-shot: she kisses him gently on the lips . . . he

gets out of the car counting rapidly.
FERDINAND : One, two, three, four, five, six, seven, eight,
nine, ten . . .
MARIANNE : And the case?
FERDINAND : On your way . . . If you have confidence . . .
you'll see . . . and me too . . .
She starts to drive her car away as FERDINAND *continues
his counting. He flings the case in the back of her car
and she drives off triumphantly.*
Interior of bowling alley. FERDINAND *has now reached
48 . . . He bowls and the camera tracks along the alley,
returning to where he is sitting. His voice counting continues over the next image of* MARIANNE.
Medium shot of MARIANNE *reconciled with her brother
at the helm of the boat. The sea glistens behind them as
they wait for the boat to leave. He takes off his sun-
glasses and they kiss affectionately. (Still on page 86)
Long-shot:* FERDINAND'S *red car arrives again outside
the closed wire gates of the little compound leading to
the jetty. He toots the horn, gets out, presses the buzzer
on the gate post, tries the gates and finds they are open.
He runs in. The keeper points to the jetty and*
FERDINAND *runs towards the boat. He shouts out to*
MARIANNE, *but he is too late. The boat is already yards
away from the quay. She stands and looks at him as he
hangs his head, and kicks his toes against the ground,
walks round in a circle foolishly, desperate and sad, de-
feated and betrayed.*
*Medium shot: he hears a strange cry and walks around
the jetty to find* DEVOS *sitting alone on the quay. They
talk and* DEVOS, *half singing, half talking, tells him the
story of the music that has haunted him all his life,
illustrating his tragic tale with elaborate gestures.*
FERDINAND : Are you okay, old chap?
DEVOS : Ah! It's that melody there . . . You've no idea what
it evokes in me . . . You can hear that melody, can't you?
FERDINAND : No, I can't hear anything.
DEVOS : Not to be believed . . . That melody, for me it's my
whole life, my whole life . . . it . . . when I hear it, for me

. . . one day, you know, I was at my place . . . it was playing . . . she was at my side . . . a woman . . . magnificent, beautiful, you understand . . . I took her hand like this . . . and then I caressed it like this . . . on top . . . on top like this. I asked her 'Do you love me?', she told me 'No ! ' and so . . . I bought the record . . . because that music for me, it had . . . it's a mass hysteria all my own . . . don't you think? . . . One day I was at my place . . . I put the record on the gramophone . . . like this . . . it was turning, turning, turning . . . in my head . . . I was dizzy! She was sitting by my side . . . it wasn't the same one, it was another . . . Ah! she wasn't as beautiful as the first one . . . at last . . . I took her hand . . . then I began to caress it . . . underneath, to change it a little. One can't always do the same thing . . . I asked her 'Do you love me?' . . . she said 'Yeah, yeah' . . . But I didn't love *her* . . . so . . . I broke the record . . . hop! la! . . . One day I turned on the radio. It was playing. That one! and why that one! instead of another? She was sitting at my side . . . she was sitting on my other side . . . because I was at her place . . . it was a third one . . . I took hold of her hand . . . and I started to caress it in both ways because I wanted to get it over and done with . . . it was starting to irritate me a bit. I asked her 'Do you love me?' She told me 'Yes, sir.' I asked her 'Will you give me your hand?' She told me, 'You've had it for the last ten minutes in your own.' It's true, believe me, it's true what I said. So, then, I kept her. Ten years! Ten years! This song, I can't take it any longer, I can't bear it any longer! You can hear it? You can hear it? . . . I can't bear it any longer, that melody. You hear it?

They both stand up and the camera pans up slightly.
FERDINAND : No.
DEVOS : That melody you hear . . . you don't hear it?
FERDINAND : Aha! No!
DEVOS : Say it . . . that I'm mad. No, but tell me immediately that I'm mad . . . go on . . . I want to hear you tell me 'You are mad.' Say it . . . 'You are mad.'
FERDINAND : You are mad.
DEVOS : Ah! well I prefer . . . I much prefer that.

101

Long-shot: FERDINAND *leaves* DEVOS *who stands alone waving his hand around his head as if to say the whole world is mad.* FERDINAND *hails a tug-boat passing close to the quay. He jumps onto it.*

FERDINAND : Are you going to the island?

PILOT : Yes, sir.

FERDINAND : What's the name of your boat?

PILOT : The *Sawoa.*

FERDINAND *makes a pun on the name* : If it's not okay it's the same price.

FERDINAND sits at the bow of the boat and lights himself a cigarette. He looks up as he hears DEVOS shouting to him from the quay.

Long-shot : DEVOS *on the quay, waving his arms around like a maniac.*

DEVOS : So, then, this music . . . that I hear, maybe it doesn't exist. This music that haunts me, which has followed me all my life . . . this tenderness, no . . . the man is not sensitive . . . you hear me? You haven't understood a thing!

Close-up of FERDINAND *looking up at the sky.*

Long-shot: FERDINAND *standing on the boat as it crosses rough seas. Grandiose romantic music.*

Long-shot jump cut. FERDINAND *reaches the top of a cliff of the island and turns and waves . . . walks along the path, singing to himself and makes the gesture with his hands, repeating* DEVOS'S *mannerisms.*

FERDINAND *singing* : ' Do you love me? '

He looks round sharply and shouts out ' Marianne! ' He runs forward. Somebody fires a gun. He fires too as he runs past a girl who walks along unperturbed. Medium close-up : FERDINAND *fires twice and shouts.*

Long-shot: FERDINAND *leaps down the trail towards a villa. In the distance* MARIANNE *and* FRED *are escaping towards the villa. (Still on page 86)* FERDINAND *fires again.*

Long-shot : he dashes round the corner of the path and we see FRED'S *body on the ground.* FERDINAND *fires again and stops.* MARIANNE *slowly stumbles down the slope towards him and falls limp into his arms. He has shot her. He starts to carry her towards the villa and we see a small neat blood-stain on her pullover in the centre of her stomach. (Still on page 87)*

FERDINAND *off*: I'm holding her close to me, and I'm crying.

MARIANNE *off*: It was the first, it was the only dream.

Medium shot: he carries her through the open door of the villa. He lays her down on a deck-chair next to the window. He comes through the open windows of the villa and picks up the telephone.

FERDINAND: Get me Paris, Mademoiselle. Balzac 75-02. Have you forgotten who Balzac was as well? Yes, yes, I'm waiting, I'm waiting . . .

He goes over to MARIANNE *and picks her up roughly. She moans . . .*

MARIANNE: I'm ill . . .

FERDINAND *carries her into the bedroom. He is talking to her as he lays her down on the bed.*

FERDINAND: This wouldn't have happened if you hadn't done that . . .

MARIANNE: Some water, please . . .

FERDINAND: This wouldn't have happened if you hadn't done that . . .

Close-up: MARIANNE *turns towards* FERDINAND. *Blood trickles from her nose and lips . . .*

MARIANNE: I ask you to forgive me, Pierrot . . .

FERDINAND *off*: My name is Ferdinand . . . It's too late.

She makes an effort but her head falls . . . her eyes are open . . . she is dead . . . (Still on page 87)

Close-up of his diary, black writing on red paper.

FERDINAND'S *diary*: ' Dynamite . . . machine guns . . . with what the two brothers must . . . to supply the rebels who . . . Marianne was saying . . . Friday . . .'

FERDINAND *is in a garage holding two strings of dynamite, when the telephone rings. He searches round until he finds the telephone and picks up the receiver.*

FERDINAND: Yes, yes, yes, yes, I am waiting, I am waiting. Balzac 75-02? Is Madame Griffon there? Is that you, Odile? Are the children well? No . . . no . . . it is not on anyone's behalf . . .

*As he is talking on the telephone, he takes some blue
paint from a tin on the shelf next to him and with a
piece of wood smears his face slowly until it is blue all
over. Close-up of the notebook. Blue paper. He inserts
the letters to complete the word ' DEATH '.*

Long-shot: FERDINAND *leaves the villa carrying with
him the two strings of dynamite. He starts to run, and
howls out two agonizing, meaningless, helpless,
anguished cries for no one to hear . . . He swings round
holding the strings of dynamite with arms outstretched
like wings, and, screaming like a fury, he dashes along
the path close to the top of the cliff.*

Close-up: FERDINAND, *sitting down, the blue paint
caked dry on his face, looks from side to side and to the
sky . . . talking to himself.*

FERDINAND : What . . . I would like to say . . . Oh! oh!
. . . why . . . after all . . . I am stupid . . .

*He gives up trying to talk and instead wraps the yellow
dynamite around his head, tying it carefully with the
long fuse. He then wraps the red dynamite around the
yellow and again ties the fuse. He takes out a box of
matches and lights a match but accidentally drops it
and the other matches scatter . . .*

FERDINAND : Oh shit ! . . . beautiful death for . . .

*Close-up of his hands grappling for the matches near
the coiled fuse wire.*

*Very long-shot: the explosion of dynamite on the top
of the cliff. (Still on page 88) The camera pans slowly
from* FERDINAND'S *violent death towards the calm open
sea . . .* MARIANNE'S *and* FERDINAND'S *voices are heard
in the last fragments of dialogue as the camera pans in
a great sweep upwards towards the sky . . . Their voices
whispering intimately together . . .*

MARIANNE *off* : She's found again . . .

FERDINAND *off* : What?

MARIANNE *off* : Eternity.

FERDINAND *off* : It is the sea . . . run away . . .

MARIANNE *off* : With the sun . . .